RED ZONE BLUES

A snapshot of Baghdad in the surge

By Pepe Escobar

NIMBLE BOOKS LLC

NIMBLE BOOKS LLC

ISBN: 978-0-9788138-9-5

Copyright 2007 Pepe Escobar

Cover photo copyright 2007 Jason Florio (http://www.floriophoto.com)

Last saved 2007-08-20.

Published by Nimble Books LLC

1521 Martha Avenue

Ann Arbor, MI 48103-5333

http://www.nimblebooks.com

Contents

About the Author

Pepe Escobar, born in Brazil in 1954, is the roving correspondent for Hong Kong/Thailand-based *Asia Times* (www.atimes.com) He has lived and worked as a foreign correspondent in London, Paris, Milan, Los Angeles and Singapore/Bangkok. Since 9/11 he has extensively covered Pakistan, Afghanistan, Central Asia, Iran, Iraq and the wider Middle East. He is the author of *Globalistan: How the Globalized World is Dissolving into Liquid War* (Nimble Books, 2007), as well as contributing editor to *The Empire and the Crescent* (published in the U.K.), *Tutto in Vendita* (published in Italy) and *Shia Power: Next Target Iran?* (published in the US/U.K.) When not on the road, he lives between Sao Paulo, Paris and Bangkok.

Preface: Play the blues

The blue light was my blues

And the red light was

my mind

    Robert Johnson, Love in Vain

The "Red Death" had long devastated the country. No pestilence had ever been so fatal, or so hideous. Blood was its Avatar and its seal—the redness and the horror of blood... But the Prince Prospero was happy and dauntless and sagacious. When his dominions were half depopulated, he summoned to his presence a thousand hale and light-hearted friends from among the knights and dames of his court, and with these retired to the deep seclusion of one of his castellated abbeys. This was an extensive and magnificent structure, the creation of the prince's own eccentric yet august taste. A strong and lofty wall girdled it in. This wall had gates of iron. The courtiers, having entered, brought furnaces and massy hammers and welded the bolts. They resolved to leave means neither of ingress or egress to the sudden impulses of despair or of frenzy from within. The abbey was amply provisioned. With such precautions the courtiers might bid defiance to contagion. The external world could take care of itself.

    Edgar Allen Poe, The Masque of the Red Death

I'd like to think of this little book as a blues compilation. It dwells on sorrow and distress—with occasional epiphanies; its protagonists are real, flesh-and-bones, struggling, suffering Iraqis; hope for them is just a tiny, distant glimmer in the (dusty) horizon. Unlike sweeping treatises on the war on Iraq, or think tank rhetorical opuses, it's much more intimate—a snapshot of life under George W. Bush's "surge," reflecting my totally unembedded visit to masque-of-the-red-death Baghdad, i.e. the Red Zone for *Asia Times* in the spring of 2007. Many of our American readers encouraged me to release the reports in book form.

This little book is also a sort of companion to my own *Globalistan*, published by Nimble Books in early 2007. *Globalistan* tracked the intersections between war and globalization, energy wars and the Pentagon's "Long War," and argued that we are already living an intestinal, undeclared, global, liquid civil war. *Red Zone Blues* illustrates its ultra-advanced battleground.

I was extremely disturbed by what I saw in Baghdad. I had been covering Iraq before, during and after 2003's Shock and Awe. Since 2005 I wanted to go back; Sunni contacts in the Red Zone told me it was suicide. I had always worked with Sunnis. But my translator had moved to Dubai (no turning back); and my driver had bought a fake Kalashnikov made in Romania for US$ 20 and joined the resistance.

So this time I worked with Shiites. This meant I could not hop on a taxi and go to the Sunni belt or the "triangle of death" as before—and not even to Shiite Najaf for that matter: as Patrick Cockburn—the best Western reporter covering the occupation on the ground—knows too well, traveling in Iraq for a lone, unembedded Western journalist is a death sentence.

I owe special thanks to *Asia Times* publisher Sondhi Limthongkul and Allen, Tony and the team in Thailand. As a journalist, I have seen my share of misery and distress—in Asia, the Middle East, Africa, South America. I left Baghdad in rage and tears. I hope *Red Zone Blues* may show why. This little book is dedicated to all Iraqis suffering on the ground and in exile; but especially to dear friend "Fatima"—a true Baghdad heroine. Now let's play the blues.

Gulf of Morbihan, Brittany, summer of 2007

A prologue: Red Zone down South

Rio de Janeiro

It's midnight on Friday at the monstrous Help disco in Copacabana, Rio's Carnival has not even started but the posse of five black brothers and a Southern whitey in NBA T-shirts fresh from Baghdad is on a mission from God—or rather King Momo (the sovereign of Carnival). The mission is as delicate as patrolling Haifa street on surge mode: but this is target identification with a twist, as the only heat-seeking missiles on view are a horde of spectacularly curvaceous Brazilian babes and uber-transvestites, ranging from coal to cream to golden hues, ready to inflict maximum damage on the "enemy." As the American wild bunch enters (screams?) Help—roughly, a larger-than-life Bangkok girlie bar set as a rollerball arena—to the sound of ear-splitting funk do morro and past a table full of Muslim Indians gone crazy on lethal *caipirinhas*, they finally reach The Green Zone: or Paradise in the Carnivalesque geopolitical scheme of things. One black brother can't help it: "Make my day, Muqtada al-Sadr!"

These "maintenance" guys on an officially-sanctioned 15-day R&R break are among hundreds of soldiers, security forces, private contractors and assorted mercenaries who have subscribed to the hottest ticket in the summer of 2007 (in the global South): Miami-based Tours Gone Wild's US$ 3000, 10-day package to Rio. And it's not only Iraq: they come all the way from Afghanistan, Central Asia and all points north and south in the worldwide empire of 700-plus US military bases. A single US soldier posted in Iraq costs US$ 390,000 a year. The war costs US taxpayers over a quarter-million dollars *a minute*. On a cost-benefit basis, Pentagon analysts might consider that with a few relaxing nights in Rio US troops in Iraq would perfect their PR, and never dream of perpetrating another Mahmoudiya, when gung-ho soldiers criminally gang-raped a teenager Iraqi girl and burned her body to bury the evidence.

1

Myself and an editor at France24—the new French 24-hour news channel—were hitting the same groove, sort of. We had had enough of tracking the Iraq quagmire, the imminent war on Iran, the latest al-Qaeda-produced al-Zawahiri rap on video. It was time to explore a new breed of combat mission. Rio—on whose beaches I spent a great deal of my teenage years—was the sexiest Red Zone on earth: a war zone in tropical paradise. Contrary to popular myth, the world is not becoming Americanized: it's being Brazilianized. What the US started to face after 9/11 has been taking place in Brazil for decades: a civil war with no front, no army, no rules and no honor.

Rio's carnival pace is as frantic as patrolling Baghdad. The jungle groove is relentless. The sensuous, steamy city is like a huge, pulsating vulva sucking everything in its stride. The headline in one of the local gory dailies unveils what goes on in the entrails of the system: "Red Command films killing of Fed and shows the video in a funk ball." The Red Command is the prime drug gang in Rio. A massive federal police force has been sent to Rio even before carnival. And funk balls—heavily controlled by the drug rings—are where the underprivileged masses get down to party.

Despite tough gun laws, gunshot victims in Brazil are in excess of 40,000 annually—four times the number in the US. Rio is undisputed Red Zone territory. "Worse than Afghanistan," say police officers. According to a UNESCO study published in early 2007, gun deaths in Brazil since 1997 topped 325,000—more than in 26 wars surveyed, including the first Gulf War and the first and second Intifadas.

℣

The Sambadrome—conceived by the late, great anthropologist Darcy Ribeiro as a stage for "the biggest popular party in the world"—is the arena for the glitzy, wealthy, sprawling Rio samba schools, which are in fact run like corporations. During Carnival week the top 13 samba schools were spending a total of almost US$ 30 million (not to mention dodgy undec-

2

lared funds) in allegories and costumes alone. The Sambadrome extravaganza is now a staple of global mainstream tourism. Meanwhile the real action—the Rio version of IEDs—is the *bloco*.

Blocos are sort of spontaneous neighborhood associations, fueled by a well-oiled marching band, whose purpose is to dress or cross-dress outrageously and hit the streets, slowly crawling from bar to bar, dancing and singing at the top of their lungs a classic repertoire of *marchinhas*. Musically, the *marchinha* ("carnival march") epitomizes what the perfect carnival tune is all about: a kind of revved-up samba with a mean break beat, hilarious horn breaks and pun-filled lyrics. At nine in the morning on Saturday, no less than 200,000 people are already massed under the scorching heat to hit the Black Ball *bloco*—a crowd three times the Sambadrome's.

Surviving Help the night before involves hours of lounging beachside protected from the scorching sun by a steady supply of fresh juices extracted from mind-blowing Amazon rainforest fruits—just in time to catch the classic Banda de Ipanema, or the healthy, typically Rio crossover of anarchism with family values. An inevitable assortment of devils, transvestites, fake office workers, the occasional Angelina Jolie and a gorgeous Miss Piggy are on show. The Band of Ipanema, founded in 1965, always mocked the Brazilian military dictatorships of the 1960s and 1970s. The front banner still reads "Yolhesman Crisbeles"—which means absolutely nothing in any language, living or dead: but for the military, that was a subversive communist code. Imagine the Pentagon reaction to a Band of Baghdad hitting the streets of Sadr City. One of the band's founders claims it is the only institution that ever worked in Brazil's colorful history—because it boasts no platform, no rules, no statutes and no boring people.

By Saturday the hefty Anglo-American contingent is also going nuts. In Bahia, Fatboy Slim gets ready to DJ on a *trio eletrico*—a lavish, truck-mounted, itinerant sound system. Brazil's Minister of Culture, iconic singer-songwriter Gilberto Gil—known in England as the "Minister of

3

Cool"—gets cozy with Quincy Jones, who's ready to do for Brazilian rhythms what he's done to Michael Jackson: he's pre-producing a documentary to be filmed in 2008 in both Rio and Bahia called *Brazilian Soul*.

Revellers are still trying to make it home—or to the beach—on Sunday morning while we, sleepy-eyed but rejuvenated by a bucket load of pineapple-with-mint nectar, are already on a mad bus ride cross town to hit another one of the 30 *blocos* of the day, the Boitata. Once again it's nine in the morning under the scorching heat—and they are all there, the guy with a knife stuck on his forehead, the transvestite dressed as a ballerina with an "I Love Jesus" T-shirt, an army of cadavers, devils, clowns, archetypal cross-dressed, wig-on, face-splattered-with-cheap-paint street revelers whose only aim in life is *cair na folia* (literally, "plunge into folly"). Top banner of the morning: "F*** Bush, let's samba."

All day Sunday—in overcrowded beaches, in bars, over the frenetic updating on the laptop of Ana Claudia Souza, the exuberant black woman who edits a celebrity website tracking all Carnival gossip in real time—the excitement inevitably converges to the Sambadrome. That's the ritual catwalk where all the cathartic myths of the Afro-Brazilian mix which the artsy tropicalist movement in the 1960s dubbed "total jelly" literally explode.

For millions in Rio living in a slum in the back of beyond and slaving away in the informal economy, like practically 50% of Brazilians, a magic 90 minutes—the time it takes for a school to cross the glamorous Sambadrome asphalt catwalk—is capable of turning anyone into King or Queen, the alter ego shining high in the altar of Carnival. One does not have to be a "highlight"—like the glittering, Hollywoodish soap opera stars and talk show hosts who headline the samba schools' parades. One just has to be a drummer in the *baterias*—the mighty, head-churning percussive factories powering the schools with the thrust of an F-16. Or a chambermaid dressed up as a Nordic deity. Thus the stirring spectacle of those working class masses arriving at the big stage on crammed buses and trains, clutching their prized costume and finishing their dress up and make up at the terminal station.

Seen from ground level, this has nothing to do with glamour. We decide to leave the Central do Brasil—Rio's shabbier, sweatier answer to New York's Grand Central station—and literally cross a border to mingle with the crowds preparing for the Big Night. On the other side, squeezed body-to-body in the dark, you are on your own. It's like leaving your Hummer or Abrams vehicle if you're a US patrol in Baghdad—as it took us just 100 meters to find out.

The IED attack happened with military precision. A foamy spray hit my face, impairing my lateral vision. As I turned around a lightning–quick hand, in a single movement, opens my zippered pocket, extracts my wallet and disappears into the crowd. My companion still clutches her backpack, but only minutes later she will find out it has also been opened, and a small purse has disappeared. The whole incident lasts less than two seconds. Those brothers at the Help disco would have been as stunned as I was. Yes, the Sunni Arab guerrilla syndrome is ubiquitous. And the message was unmistakable: you, gringos, don't belong here, but to the free champagne-flowing VIP booths at US$ 800 a pop (the Rio equivalent of the Green Zone). As in black American ghetto folklore, "the Man control the day, but we control the night."

It could have been worse—like getting popped and showing up post-mortem as a video in a funk ball. We had just been added to the average 128 (registered) muggings a day in Rio—as we learn a while later in Rio's 6th police precinct. The precinct is on a roll: the investigators are working a non-stop 24-hour shift, before midnight more than thirty people have already been arrested, and five dodgy characters are laid out on the dirty floor before me as an identification line up—alleged members of a pick-pocket ring. Jose Carlos Esch, the weary inspector in charge, answers non-stop calls of journalists who want to know about a homicide ("It was not here"). As he types our report number 006-00757/2007, suddenly we hear fireworks. No, it's not Baghdad: it's celebration for one of the samba schools finishing their parade. The police inspector climbs up from his seat, opens the window and the three of us stay there, in silence, like in a Fellini movie, staring at the arabesques in the sky. A few feet away, the five dangerous but frightened criminals await someone to go medieval on them as no loot has been found in their possession.

And then there was the clincher. Walking back to the station—without bothering to stay and watch the parade—some quick hand in the mass body-to-body friction even tried to steal a flask of liquor from my back pocket. "This is *very* wild," murmurs my companion. Geopolitical message: the underprivileged masses of the global South are desperate, and ready to do anything to just survive. Undocumented, un-credit carded and flat broke, I felt just like one of them.

So the next day we did what we had to do. Before, once again as journalists, succumbing to the demented flow of non-stop breaking news, we paid a Nietzschean homage to the death of all idols—God, Motherland, Revolution—and sang the body electric: we joined one more *bloco*—loosely translatable as the "Suck but don't Drool"—and sang a thousand *marchinhas* at the top of our lungs. If only Bush and Muqtada al-Sadr could join us.

1: In the heart of Little Fallujah

Damascus

> *Today's "zero point" returns Iraq to its own history, a history written with the ashes of incendiary fires, with its sons fleeing in all directions on the one hand, and its exiles returning to their own homes on the other. I truly do not know if distance today can be defined through the experiences of refugees, or the masses of displaced people, or the exiles returning to burning cities to live out a sense of loss. Distances begin to take on the forms of lines which have been drawn on ashen roads, resembling the traces of people who have lost their way and have never arrived.*
>
> *Mohamed Mazloom, Baghdad poet, born 1963, exiled in Syria*

This is biblical exodus—the YouTube version. Welcome to Little Fallujah—previously Geramana, southeast Damascus. The Nahda area of Geramana now boasts at least 200,000 resident Iraqis. They visibly came with all their savings—and made good use of it. The congested main drag of al-Nahda is an intoxicating apotheosis of anarchic capitalism, business piled upon business—Hawaii fruits, Galilia underwear, Call Me mobile, Snack Bambino, Discovery software school, Eva sunglasses, boutique Tout le Monde, all Iraqi-owned.

Street banners promote nightly Iraqi music festivals. Iraqi restaurants rule—such as the favorite Iraqi Palm Tree, with piped bird-singing and a flotilla of Chevy Suburbans with red Iraqi license plates at the door, also popular with Syrians, Lebanese and Palestinians from refugee camps and even Somali and Sudanese immigrants. According to a resident, "Druze beautiful girls" in the neighborhood have been replaced by "fat Iraqi men"—a reference to when al-Nahda used to be a little Druze village sprinkled with a few Christians.

7

A 100-square-meter apartment sells for 2 million Syrian pounds (roughly US$40,000)—four times as much as before the Iraqi invasion. One square meter in prime business premises is now US$20,000. Iraqis always pay US dollars cash. No wonder the price of potatoes has also risen fourfold. Not to mention the inflation of hairdressing salons—where Mesopotamian sirens perfect their Christina Aguilera-influenced, multi-shaded pompadours. And right beside al-Nahda is the action—al-Rahda, peppered with smart cafes like the Stop In and al-Nabil, both not far away from a huge, stern Sunni mosque.

There's not only Little Fallujah. There are also Little Baghdad, Little Mosul, Little Babylon, Little Najaf. Exile replicates the stark divide found in Baghdad. Middle-class Sunnis won't be seen around the middle-class Shiites who tend to go to the area around the spectacular Sayyida Zaynab shrine—a key Shiite pilgrim site boasting distinctive Persian architecture that would be perfectly at home in Qom or Mashhad. This area is Little Najaf. The stories, though, are similar to Little Fallujah's. Shiite families had to abandon their homes in predominantly Sunni neighborhoods in Iraq—otherwise they would have been killed. They came, they saw, they opened a restaurant, and they're in business.

This proliferation of Little Iraqs accounts for the biggest exodus in the Middle East since the Palestinians were forced to abandon their own lands in 1948 as the State of Israel was being created. In every single month in Iraq at least 40,000 people become displaced. According to the United Nations High Commission for Refugees (UNHCR), there may be as many as 50,000 a month. Were that rate to continue, before 2020 all the population of Iraq would have been "liberated" from its own country.

In northern Damascus, a crammed room inside the Iraqi Embassy compound is pure Dante's purgatory—waves and waves of Iraqis desperately in search of the right missing papers to request political asylum in a Western embassy. Thousands may be planning to stay in Syria, but for the great majority the promised land really means a visa for Canada, Australia or the ever-elusive European Union.

Whichever Iraq one picks in Damascus, the mantra is recited in unison. Any glimmer of hope for the future hinges on the Americans leaving—and the establishment, by Iraqis, with no foreign interference, of a non-sectarian government.

Take Nabir, owner of the Salon Musa, a barbershop decorated with a giant poster of soccer star Ronaldinho in a Nike-sponsored Brazilian yellow jersey. Call him the Barber of Fallujah. His family left Turkey in the early 20th century. Nabir left Iraq in late 2004. He stresses that "during Saddam, everybody had work, and everything worked." After a stint at the former Saddam International Airport, he worked for the Americans as a barber in—where else?—Fallujah. His hopes are "that the country will be totally destroyed, and only Iraqis will be allowed to come back." He was against the war. He left because his family had no security. And he does not want to go back.

The story of Aziz Abu Ammar, an affable sexagenarian impeccably dressed with suit and silk tie, is emblematic of what happened to Iraq's professional and cultural elites. We talk at the most spectacular of settings, inside the Umayyad mosque just after evening prayers. Ammar is a retired government official from the Ministry of Economy and Trade. He sold everything in his native Baghdad—except his house—and left with his whole family in late 2006, "because of the bombings," mirroring a detailed survey by the International Organization for Migration (IOM) according to which most Iraqis leave after their lives are directly threatened.

Ammar is emphatic: "There is no Sunni against Shiite. The Americans provoked it. Since the beginning they started talking about separate areas. In Baghdad most marriages are mixed." That's exactly his case. He is Shiite, his wife is Sunni. He says that "in all Arab countries we feel comfortable," but anyway he has entered a demand for a long-term visa to Australia. "We don't want to put pressure on the kindness of the Syrian people."

The solution for Iraq is "the Americans out, all foreign troops out. But even after they leave, we will need a strongman. I don't trust any of these political parties or groups. The only solution would be new, really free elections." He insists "al-Qaeda destroyed the country," but in the same breath adds, "al-Qaeda is an American creation." Shiite cleric Muqtada al-Sadr may not be the solution either: "He's too young, has a lot to learn. His father [the late Grand Ayatollah Mohammad Sadiq al-Sadr] was good."

It's easy to forget that Hafez Assad's Syria and Saddam Hussein's Iraq had no diplomatic relations whatsoever from 1980 to 1997. Now every Iraqi showing up at the Syrian border automatically gets a one-month visa; they then apply for a three-month resident visa. Visa runs are common. Unlike in "liberated" Iraq, in Syria there's virtually no unemployment for Iraqis. Overqualified, young, educated Iraqis at least survive with dignity as internet-cafe managers or restaurant waiters. Iraqis are admitted to Syrian schools and universities with no special prerequisites. The Syrian state pays half of their medical bills. No wonder there is also a boom in mixed Syrian-Iraqi marriages.

Compare this situation with Jordan, which has become a de facto Hashemite kingdom of refugees—first the Palestinians after 1948 and now no fewer than 1 million Iraqis, almost 20% of the total population of 5.5 million. But unlike Syria, US-backed Jordan now is not exactly exhibiting its welcoming face. Iraqis in Syria swear that only the sick and the elderly are allowed to cross the border into Jordan. Soon Iraqis may be barred from buying property. Collective-taxi drivers plying the infested-with-bandits Amman-Baghdad highway say that Jordanian police constantly repatriates busloads of Iraqi refugees to the border: they are in fact treated as illegal immigrants. Unlike in Syria, they don't have the right to work, have no discount on medical expenses, and can't even put their kids in school.

Little Iraqs are now part of the latest layer superimposed on Damascus—arguably the oldest city in the world (Aleppo in northern Syria begs to differ). And this after the low skyline saturated with prehistoric terrestrial aerials and rusty satellite dishes was superimposed on the narrow, medieval lanes and alleys of the fabulous Old City. Syrians are in essence very proud and very honest—as are Iraqis. As the calcified Syrian regime remains immersed in corruption, for real people corruption works out merely as a survival tactic—as it did and still does for Iraqis.

The inflation of trendy girls from Mesopotamia may have contributed to an inflation of *lanjeri* (lingerie) boutiques side-by-side with shops selling veils, not only in Little Fallujah but in the venerable, monstrous souq al-Hamidiyah. The mix is terrific: chador on show, made-in-China silk bikini underneath. The best clients happen to be from the Maghreb region in Northern Africa.

All roads do lead to Damascus. One day even Armani-suited, Hermes scarf-enveloped Madam Speaker Nancy Pelosi showed up, discreetly touring the Old City by night before her meeting the next morning with President Bashar al-Assad. Pelosi did not play the scratchy White House CD according to which "Syria is a supporter of terrorism." So she might have had time for a little meditation on an empire fading—as the souq magically merges with the remains of the western gate of the 3rd-century Roman temple of Jupiter and opens the view to the fabulous Umayyad mosque with its courtyard, like in a psychedelic dream, converging all the faiths, all the colors and all the accents of the world.

Syria recognizes—formally—that Iraqis are refugees who need to be protected. The Bush administration, on the other hand, could never admit to the world it is the source of all this—"the fastest-growing refugee crisis in the world" as defined by Kenneth Bacon, president of Refugees International. Madam Speaker would have learned much more about the cataclysmic effects of the war on Iraq—and what Syria is actually doing about it—if she had traded the historic wonders of the Old City for a stroll in all-too-real Little Fallujah.

2: Night bus from Baghdad

The road from Damascus to Attanf, on the Syrian/Iraqi border, is pure Desolation Row. Scattered nomad shepherds search precious grasslands for their flock. An incoming, rickety Nissan bus from Iraq passes by, loaded with goods but carrying only four people. A pair of rusty Soviet-era missiles is transported by a slow military truck—to be positioned at the border in a face-off with the Americans?

There are three major crossing points from Syria to Iraq: Al Yarubiye in the northeast, Al Bukamal and Attanf. Attanf, the village, consists of three bombed-out houses. The border itself is just a customs and immigration post. The arrival of a stranger provokes quite a commotion—like in a Sergio Leone western. In typical police state style, at the dingy immigration control room everyone is afraid to talk. No one speaks a single word in any foreign language. An Iraqi doctor, a woman, fleeing hell in Baghdad and about to become the newest refugee in Syria, is brought in a hurry to mediate. No one will talk without an express authorization from "Damascus"—this remote, wrathful entity beyond human understanding.

The Iraqi refugees are quite straightforward, though. Yes, there are only American soldiers on the other side, 7 km of no man's land away, a true measure of Iraq's "sovereignty." Yes, they may hold cars and trucks coming from Syria for many hours, sometimes even a day, before letting them through. Yes, they look for young men who may be potential jihadis. Yes, the road is dangerous but not as dangerous as Amman-Baghdad. And most of all *Inch'Allah*—they finally made it, in safety.

During the spring of 2007 the White House and the State Department were still insisting that Syria allows and/or encourages jihadis to cross their border into Iraq—going as far as stating that 90% of the suicide bombers in Iraq have crossed from Syria. They seemed to ignore Col. William Crowe, the Pentagon official in charge of all those Americans on the Iraqi side of the border, who said on the record there is "no large influx of foreign fighters." Moreover that wrathful entity, "Damascus," had repeatedly confirmed most of the 724 km-long border had been fitted with barbed wire and reinforced sand barriers—and no less than 1500 potential jihadis had been captured or deported.

But the fact is any enterprising jihadi with a GPS and minimal tribal connections could and still can engage in cross-border at his will. In theory, "Damascus," from President Bashar al-Assad on down, is interested in combating smuggling and jihadi traffic. The devil is in the details—how the Syrian police/military hierarchy actually deals with the problem.

For starters, Syrian business is in the hands of a powerful Sunni oligarchy. They will obviously be tempted to lend a hand to their Sunni *muqawama* (resistance) brothers in the east. Syrian military forces at wasteland border points—like in Attanf—consist of no more than a few bored men with rifles. Corruption is the norm. Evading surveillance is a matter of walking a few kilometers in the desert.

Historically, Iran, Iraq and Syria were united by the Silk Road. Attanf, for instance, is not very far from fabled Palmyra. The interaction has never ceased. Nowadays we may be seeing a new Silk Road pipeline—not only of men, ideas and commerce but also weapons. Whatever comes from Iran has to pass through Iraq and Syria to reach Lebanon (Hezbollah) and Palestine (Hamas). Same for Sunni solidarity, either from Lebanon or from Syria. expressed in Iraq via men, ideas, commerce or weapons.

Accusing Syria of being a suicide bomber factory is nonsense. The absolute majority of suicide bombers in Iraq are Saudis, and they crossed from US-ally Saudi Arabia. Syria, since the fall of Baghdad in April 2003, may have witnessed an inflation of Islamists, nationalists and former Ba'ath supporters of Saddam. For the Syrian government, having their own Islamists crossing the border to fight the Americans in Iraq has always sounded like a good idea: a way of sweeping a problem under someone else's carpet. But to imply that Syria has become a sanctuary of Islamic fundamentalists and radical Ba'athists at the same time is also nonsense.

଼ଚ

Not many jihadis take the night bus to Baghdad, but thousands of Iraqi families did take the night bus from Baghdad. Middle-class Iraqi Sunnis who have made it through the Syrian-Iraqi border tend to establish themselves in areas like Little Fallujah. For lower-middle-class Iraqi Shiites the favored area is around the spectacular, Persian style Sayyida Zaynab shrine, in southeast Damascus, with its turquoise arabesques and glittering geometrical mirrors. Inside, pilgrims from Iran, Afghanistan and Central Asia mingle with mullahs and *hojjatoleslam*, praying for hours or just meditating. There's always a whiff of perfume in the air.

But outside everything revolves around the war on Iraq. In a small shop owned by the Damistani family from Bahrain, in front of the renamed, derelict Iraqi Square, facing a huge street banner which would be prime Pentagon target practice (both Assads, father Hafez and son Bashar, alongside Hezbollah's Sheikh Nasrallah), a loquacious girl and a burly man come to grips with the Iraqi side of the road ("Commandos abduct people," she says; "It happens sometimes," he adds; "The Americans can stop our buses for one or two days," she tries to prevail; "No, they stop the bus only at the border, and then in front of Abu Ghraib," he mumbles). They sell bus tickets to Baghdad. A one-way ticket costs 900 Syrian pounds (roughly US$ 18). In the "busy" season—i.e., the summer of 2006—it was 1500 Syrian pounds. The lone bus departs at 9:00 pm and, depending on the collective good karma, arrives the next day at 5:00 pm. The same trip on a GMC truck would cost at least US$50 per person.

Way before Bush's surge, by the end of 2005, traveling was "safe." Now it's "not safe." A glance at the log says it all: there's only one registered passenger for tonight's bus. Virtually all passengers are Iraqis—unwilling returnees because they ran out of money. There is also the odd Iranian, trying to make his dangerous way to Najaf. Every passenger coming from Baghdad, they say, arrives petrified with fear but thanking Allah for having escaped in one piece.

The neighborhood around Sayyida Zaynab is lower proletarian poor—far from the dusty glitz of Little Fallujah. As many as 60,000 Iraqis are now residents. At the Al Kazimiyah shop Imad, formerly a math teacher in Baghdad, has practically given up on selling bus tickets. His salary is US$100 a month, but he is spending US$300 on his family of four since he arrived in late 2006. He confirms thousands of families are running out of money, and will have to go back. He is hoping for "Baghdad to get better" to go home, but harbors no illusions. His wife's brother has a British passport. He has entered a visa application for England. But he would be more than happy to relocate anywhere in the world.

Outside on the dusty road a man is wailing. He is actually speaking, but not on camera, to a Syrian TV crew. He thanks President Bashar for his hospitality towards all Iraqis, and he blames all Iraq's problems on "Amrika, Israel and the Mossad"—not before stressing there was never any problem in Iraq between Sunnis and Shiites. Nearby, in an improvised bakery—basically a stone oven—a man with a disconcerting smile is producing sublime bread with capsicum. He arrived at the neighborhood just before the surge, with his whole family. The baker of Baghdad actually has a degree "in technology studies." But what matters is that he survived Baghdad, and that night bus from Baghdad—so his smiles of joy had to be imprinted in the daily little miracle of baking the perfect bread.

3: The Baghdad gulag

There are three overlapping wars in Iraq: the Sunni Arab guerrilla against the US; strands of the Sunni Arab guerrilla against assorted Shiite militias/death squads; and al-Qaeda in Iraq/The Islamic State of Iraq against the US-backed Iraqi government at the Green Zone. Make it four wars: the Sunni Arab guerrilla against the government *inside* the Green Zone. Better yet, make it five wars: the Sadrists, from Sadr City to Kufa and Najaf, against the Americans.

All strands of these five overlapping wars will never allow the Bush administration—or Anglo-American Big Oil—to control Iraq's oil wealth. Were the new oil law to be ratified by the Iraqi Parliament, implementation will be a certified nightmare, and security for billions of dollars of necessary investment non-existent. Strands of these five overlapping wars also will never accept the long-term imposition of vast US military bases under a Status of Forces Agreement (SOFA) negotiated with dodgy politicians who spend more time in London than in Baghdad.

Setting a precise date for a total US withdrawal—the crystal clear demand insistently formulated by Muqtada al-Sadr —would be the only way for the Bush administration to salvage a modicum of not totally humiliating defeat. Instead, as the spring of 2007 glided by, the world was told to get ready for the imminent arrival of the Baghdad gulag.

No realist in his right mind could possibly ignore the 14-km-long throngs compacted all along the Kufa to Najaf road at the fourth anniversary of the fall of Baghdad; hundreds of thousands, perhaps more than a million Iraqi nationalists, waving Iraqi flags—with no room for religious divide—responding to Muqtada al-Sadr's call of "Occupation out!" This Shiite Million Man March proved once again Sadrists rule the Shiite street—and are the most powerful political force among Iraqi Shiites. Yet for the Bush administration Muqtada al-Sadr—as every nationalist with immense popular appeal—continued to be nothing but an evildoer who must be squashed by all counterinsurgency means necessary.

Imperial and neocolonial systems are incapable of thinking laterally. The French didn't in Algeria. The Americans didn't in Vietnam. The Israelis didn't in Palestine. The Americans didn't again in Iraq; call it counterinsurgency run amok. 30 of Baghdad's 89 districts were supposed to become gated communities from hell—cellophane-wrapped compounds where only Iraqis with a new, theoretically safe ID will be allowed in and out of this "secure environment," in Pentagon newspeak. Yes, it would be Orwellian. Better yet, it would be a post-mod, Arab condo version of Jeremy Bentham's *Panopticon*, where the eye of the system is ubiquitous.

In the last chapter of my book *Globalistan*—titled *Condofornia vs. Slumistan*—I argue that the future now revolves around the tension between gated communities and unruly slums, "secure environments" and black waves of anger. Wherever both meet—from Baghdad to Rio or Sao Paulo, Brazil—we may see endless replays of *Black Hawk Down*. The Baghdad gulag is a Pentagon-enforced Condofornia imposed over an Arab Slumistan. May no one be fooled: it's being conducted as a technical experiment, with live Iraqis as guinea pigs, and bound to be replicated in other areas of the Pentagon-created "arc of instability" from the Andes to the horn of Africa to Arabia to Central Asia.

May no one be fooled (again): guerrillas will IED the system from their underground cells; and many a Black Hawk will go down. But as everyone will be watching the destined-to-failure experiment, really serious matters—like three new, crucial American mechanized brigades deploying east of Baghdad on the way to be strategically positioned at the Iraqi-Iranian border—will be taking place in the cover of night.

The Sunni Arab *muqawama* celebrated the arrival of the Baghdad gulag by attacking the heart of the system itself, the Green Zone. The bomb that exploded in the cafeteria of the Baghdad Convention Center—which houses the Iraqi Parliament, inside the Green Zone—was yet another crystal-clear message: we can strike you as we please, and where we please. It's been an open secret in Baghdad for months that strands of the *muqawama* boast they can sweep over the Green Zone and decimate the innocuous al-Maliki government whenever they choose to.

The Green Zone bomb at the Parliament cafeteria was metaphorical in more ways than one. This was already a bombed-out Iraqi Parliament. Sadrists, holding 32 seats, were threatening a boycott. Unlike throngs of SCII, Da'wa and Kurd parliamentarians who prefer to watch Chelsea matches in London drinking vintage scotch, Sadrists actually go to work every day in the Green Zone. If the Sadrists and the Islamic Virtue Party representatives actually decided to boycott, as well as the hardcore Sunni members of the Iraqi Accord Front, this Parliament would be no more.

Crucially, this would mean no passing of the Holy of the Holies, the new Iraqi oil law. By April 2007 it was an open secret in Baghdad—as well as among Iraqi refugees in Damascus—that the Bush administration's famous "benchmarks" to the al-Maliki government revolved around oil: if the oil law is not approved, "all options are on the table," and that would mean a white coup with the re-installation of former CIA asset, former interim prime-minister, former "butcher of Fallujah" Iyad Allawi, whose main task would be... to get the oil law approved.

A Sunni Arab refugee businessman in Little Fallujah, now running a kebab joint and counting every Syrian pound, summed it all up: "The bomb could have killed them all, these politicians. We are not sorry. They are just adding more misery to the Iraqi people. Nothing will change if the Americans don't leave." He is Sunni. And he agrees with Muqtada al-Sadr.

So much for sectarian civil war. For the 1.2 million-plus Iraqi refugees in Syria, Sunnis in Little Fallujah or Shiites around Sayyida Zaynab, the verdict is unanimous: with a population descended to Fourth World status, infant mortality doubling, 60% unemployment, a refugee crisis and the ground zero of civil society, there's only one answer: Americans out. Muqtada al-Sadr knows it. Instead, soon on every screen, ready for the summer blockbuster season, we were about to watch the latest Pentagon production: the Baghdad gulag.

4: We build walls, not nations

By the spring of 2007, no British soccer players, Czech supermodels or Chinese infotainment moguls were lining up to get a piece of the new exclusive gated territory in the global market—courtesy of Pentagon real-estate developers and lavishly promoted as The Great Wall of Adhamiyah.

But then, who wants to live behind a 5-km-long, 3.7-meter-high concrete wall, being erected in haste by the 407th Brigade support battalion of the famed 82nd Airborne Division, currently based in sprawling Camp Taji, north of Baghdad.

It was being built, Dubai-style, by semi-slave labor—underpaid Iraqi crews, although the engineers and the cranes are all-American. And when ready, what's inside—the Sunni neighborhood of Adhamiyah—would look exactly its same sorry self: no cappuccino al fresco Starbucks style, no Versace outlets, no fit blondes on in-line skates.

No wonder Pentagon "engineers"—imperiously impervious to irony—had been mumbling about how the local population would react to their new development. Iraqi Prime Minister Nouri al-Maliki expressed his "concern," calling for construction to be halted. The US military did not say whether it would comply.

So here it was—the first installment of the Baghdad gulag; apartheid in Mesopotamia, or Balkanization with Arabic subtitles.

"Suicide bombers" and/or "death squads"—whose life, according to the Pentagon, would be "more difficult" with the arrival of the gated community, celebrated by lobbying a few Katyusha rockets inside the walled-off area. Similarities with the wall being built by Israel in the Palestinian West Bank are also to the point: no concrete wall peppered with checkpoints would be able to block the main fact that every hour in Iraq, day in, day out, there are at least seven or eight bloody bombings or attacks, 75% of them against the US occupation, 17% of them against the so-called Iraqi security forces.

The US cannot cut off the head of the (resistance) snake in Iraq—simply because there is no head: a Buddhist monk would say the snake now is one with the river itself, and it flows non-stop. Walls are irrelevant—either to the resistance or to militias or death squads.

Already by April 2007 the surge promoted by George W. Bush was no more—its metaphorical wall smashed by almost one hundred car and truck bombings since February, perpetrated either by strands of the Sunni Arab resistance, some more nationalistic, some more Islamic, or by al-Qaeda in the Land of the Two Rivers.

If walls were such a brilliant idea—as Pentagon "engineers" didn't seem to remember one in Berlin—then why didn't neo-cons of the then French presidential candidate Nicolas Sarkozy variety propose walling inner Paris from the suburban Islamic throngs that invade it every weekend? Oops, maybe because recent Europol research on Islamic terrorism in the European Union had detected only one Islamic terror attack in the EU in 2006 among 498 incidents.

In the meantime nine leading Sunni Arab resistance groups, including the Jaysh Ansar al-Sunna, the 1920 Revolution Brigades and the Islamic Front for the Iraqi Resistance—all with no "foreign" connections, meaning basically al-Qaeda—united all their know-how against three very clear enemies: the US occupation, the inefficient, corrupt al-Maliki government, and al-Qaeda in the Land of the Two Rivers.

According to all recent polls, 80% of Iraqis are against the occupation: this includes virtually all the Sunnis—including those in the Adhamiyah gated area—and more than 70% of Shiites. Sixty percent of all Iraqis think the US controls everything in Iraq; no wonder, when gated areas are erected without consulting the local population, or when the key security agency—the dreaded Iraqi National Intelligence Service—is basically a phenomenally expensive CIA asset (US$3 billion already consumed in less than three years).

Instead of building gated areas, the leading Sunni Arab resistance groups wanted to talk real business. They duly laid out their conditions for—among other things—not bombing any future Pentagon real-estate projects.

They wanted direct negotiations with General David Petraeus, the Pentagon supremo in Iraq, and the US Embassy in the (walled, but breachable) Green Zone. They wanted Washington to drop the al-Maliki government (that was more or less on the way). And they wanted two things they know they will never get: financial compensation for all the horrors inflicted on Iraq since the 2003 invasion (maybe they should request a meeting with Iraq liberator-in-chief Paul Wolfowitz after he quit the World Bank in disgrace); and the smashing of all L. Paul Bremer's neo-liberal laws, especially making sure that Iraq's oil wealth will not be sold out to Anglo-American Big Oil.

The Bush administration would obviously say no to most, if not all, of these conditions. What's left couldn't be anything other than building exclusive gated areas. The *muqawama,* for its part, didn't stop. By the summer of 2007 three of the key Sunni guerrilla groups—the 1920 Revolution Brigades, Ansar al-Sunna and Iraqi Hamas—had formed the Political Office for the Iraqi Resistance, a public political alliance to basically throw out all occupation troops, block any collaboration with occupation-endorsed political institutions, and declare null and void any agreement between the US and the Iraqi government.

This was a sort of "shadow cabinet"—without formal support from any Arab government (for example Saudi Arabia or Syria); without any funding from Iran; without any links with Shiite religious parties or militias; and without any links with al-Qaeda in the Land of the Two Rivers. Abu Ahmad, spokesman for Iraqi Hamas, confirmed that within the resistance, the consensus was that the Americans would "start to withdraw" by the summer of 2008. These were the new "facts on the ground" on the Sunni side of the street.

5: "All life is waiting"

Only her eyelashes can be seen in profile, fluttering obsessively like the wings of a butterfly. She is like her own striking, svelte Kaaba, surrounded by an ocean of pilgrims—full black elegantly draped chador over jeans and a discreet mauve pair of pointy shoes, full *hijab*, only the heavily kohl-rimmed eyelashes trying to decode the torn-down messages in Arabic script, and then the official's request for a pile of abstruse documents. Inevitably she has to sit down, like everyone else, in the antechamber of purgatory—the cramped, dingy room of the consular section at the Iraqi Embassy in Damascus.

Her first words, when she breaks her silence, are "Waiting ... All life is waiting." Then her story shapes around familiar contours.

She is a young, educated, skilled professional—a veterinarian from Baghdad. Her husband "was killed" two months ago, she says with an almost imperceptible shrug, as if it were self-evident. By her side sits her six-year-old kid, frightened look, hair plastered with gel and wearing sunglasses. Her little daughter was left behind in Baghdad, with her family.

In a less harsh universe she would have been the female lead in a Hollywood tearjerker—those kohl-rimmed eyelashes under the black-veiled face filling the screen, and the audience, with awe. In unforgiving real life she is just one more Iraqi refugee—one more whose story will never make it to the front pages of US corporate newspapers or be carefully re-enacted by glamorous Diane Sawyer lookalikes.

The inflow through the dingy room is relentless—from grandmas who seem to have just sprung up from the kitchen to aged peasants who've been sporting the same coat for decades, from housewives in white scarves and plastic sandals dragging their reluctant children to sheikhs in fine blue robes with golden cufflinks, golden watch and golden mobile phones. All are equal in the face of distress. Occasionally, a chador-clad woman—a war widow—breaks down into pungent wailing: she cannot produce the stamp, the seal or the piece of paper the bureaucracy demands. When a small wooden window is closed—distress has to be meticulously processed—the men protest in vain to the fully made-up official in dressed-to-kill mode.

A mom and daughter are also waiting. They look like an average mom and daughter from Queens in New York or Camden Town in London. But Mom is visibly about to give it all up and collapse, and daughter tries all she can to maintain their dignified composure. Their house was destroyed by a car bomb on New Year's Eve in Baghdad (eight people died). Mom reaches for her purse to show the dog-eared photos. The bomb was aimed at a restaurant.

They miraculously escaped because they were in the back yard. Now the head of the family, a sexagenarian, is ill and cannot find work. "Nobody helps us. They destroyed our country. Why? Why?" They are aiming for a visa to the United States. "Impossible." Too many pieces of paper to collect. Mom warns, "Believe me, there are at least 6 million of us like this"—a reference to the millions of currently displaced Iraqis.

Suddenly an eerie silence envelops the squalid room. Business is closed for the day. More protestations. So much distress, so much paperwork to fill, so little time. The lucky ones will have to come back in a day, or two or many, to another window through another gate, and be crammed by the hundreds, called by name for hours on end to collect the stamp, seal or document that might open a small window of hope. "My friend has a company in Guangzhou." "Is it better to try for a Spanish visa, or for Portugal?" "Don't try Australia, you will wait forever."

The striking veterinarian widow would like to resettle in England. But tomorrow night she will only make it to the lone night bus to Baghdad, where she hopes to rescue her little daughter, and then, back to Syria, resigned to keep waiting, waiting, waiting for a glimpse of what life might have been.

I never saw her again.

6: Fear and loathing in the Red Zone

Baghdad

There must be some way to get out of here
Said the joker to the thief
There's too much confusion
I can't get no relief

Bob Dylan, All Along the Watchtower

It's noon on Sunday right in front of the Adhamiyah wall—the now in-famous symbol of the Pentagon-devised Baghdad gulag. On Muhamad al-Kasem highway, a few battered cars and vans stop, their occupants curious to examine this prime stretch of "ghettoization."

Behind lies Adhamiyah, one the key arteries of the Red Zone and privi-leged heartland of Sunni Arab guerrillas. The streets are littered with all sorts of debris, some blocked by tanks, some blocked by the usual blast wall slalom. The road to Abu Hanifa Mosque—where the Sunni Arab resistance was born on April 8, 2003, a little over a week after the "libera-tion" of Baghdad—is also blocked. It was in Abu Hanifa that a 3,000-strong demonstration assembled a few days ago to protest against the wall. Adhamiyah is virtually encircled by US forces, but for fear of constant attacks their checkpoints are always mobile.

A few minutes later we are still close to the heart of Adhamiyah, on al-Mashatil Road, one of its main streets. We are unembedded, non-Hummer convoy-transported, non-Kevlar protected, and not surrounded by 100 soldiers and circled overhead by three Black Hawks and two Apaches, like US presidential candidate John MacCain in his recent visit ("Hello, habibi!") to Shorja market (the next day 21 merchants and workers at the market were ambushed and murdered). We are just three journalists—two Iraqis, "Abdel" and "Fatima" (their real identities should be protected) and myself, the foreigner with his head in a red keffiah, all aboard a civilian white Toyota stuck in traffic.

There's a checkpoint ahead. Incoming traffic has to slow down in front of a Hummer of the Iraqi Defense Forces. A soldier is talking to the driver of a van. Suddenly there is a shot. The soldier falls to the ground, right before our eyes, screaming in pain. He is not dead instantly. His companion, by the Hummer, takes some time to react, then also starts shooting. People duck in their cars; street wisdom is that if these were US troops, they would be shooting at random and every car would be sprayed with bullets.

Some cars hit reverse and join our traffic flow. Chador-clad women pedestrians speed across the boulevard in panic. At first we thought the shot came from a sniper on the roof of a house on our side of the boulevard. But sniper shots are silent. Soon we realize the Iraqi soldier may have been shot from a passing car. Abdel quips, "If we had this image, AP would buy it for US$ 100,000." Welcome to Adhamiyah.

Ten minutes later, we are arrested.

The day had already started under high tension, as US jets around 9:00 am bombed positions supposedly held by al-Qaeda in Iraq/Islamic State of Iraq guerrillas in explosive Dora, south Baghdad. We stop by the recently bombed Sarafiya bridge over the Tigris, which links the al-Qasra side of Sunni Adhamiyah to Shiite al-Altafiyah.

Residents are adamant: the bomb was planted "by the Americans"; one of them says, "The night before the bombing, the Americans were surrounding the bridge, and right after the bomb exploded, we heard the noise of a jet." If this is true, it would fit a perceived—by a overwhelming majority of Sunnis and Shiites alike—American strategy of inciting sectarian war: Shiites are now forced to pass through turbulent Adhamiyah if they want to go, for instance, to al-Mustansariyah University (also recently bombed), which is considered in Baghdad as a "Shiite" university.

We are stuck yet again in a hellish traffic jam, in the Bab al-Madam area, before a checkpoint at the Ministry of Health. It's an ultra-sensitive area—scene of many battles between US forces and the Sunni Arab resistance. Suddenly, a very bad move: a policeman spots a foreign-looking individual ("You look Iranian") in a car with a video camera. Police at this stretch are all from Shiite cleric Muqtada al-Sadr's Mahdi Army. In their minds this instantly means spying. The Iraqi journalists produce their credentials to no avail. Cries of *"Sahafa!"* ("journalists") don't cut it. We—and the camera—are in fact apprehended by the Mahdi Army. Abdel goes to the ministry to try to solve the problem.

Meanwhile, Fatima's glitzy black Nokia goes missing. After some waiting, we are also summoned to the first floor bureau of Abu Sama, head of security and also spokesman for the ministry. There are posters of Muqtada and Imam Hussein everywhere. Security at the ministry is all Mahdi Army. The minister is a Sadrist himself. If we had the chance to go to one of the upper floors we would be able to see, through the windows, open-air autopsies performed on the ground at the neighboring Baghdad morgue.

The tortuous ensuing conversation is like a dadaist manifesto. Abu Sama—and his attending score of assistants and policemen—turn the whole episode into a diatribe against the evils of Saddam Hussein, while suggesting Fatima's phone was not really stolen, and examining the guilty images in the camera with barely a passing glance.

They are all southern Shiites—from Najaf, Diwaniyah, Nassiriyah— more eager to display their tribal affiliation as a badge of honor than discussing the incident. It all finishes with excuses ("people here at the ministry are very tense"), cups of tea and invitations to visit again. Abdel then reveals what really happened.

At checkpoints, the Mahdi Army often provokes some confusion so as to have mobile phones stolen: this is a business. But in the case of the camera, the threat to us was real. Abdel happened to have installed a radio station in Sadr City, so he knows key Mahdi Army officials. Otherwise, he said, we would have been branded as "spies" and shot on sight. Right by the curbside. Just like the soldier at the checkpoint. We would thus join the ranks of the 188 journalists—and counting—killed since the "liberation" in 2003.

A few minutes later we learn that the very popular Amal al-Mudarris, 58, host of the top radio show Studio Asha, aired every day at 10am, has been the victim of an assassination attempt in al-Khadraa, west Baghdad. She survived.

The hundreds of thousands of Iraqis killed since April 2003, the more than four million exiled and internally displaced, the overlapping ethnic cleansing neighborhood by neighborhood, the abysmal impotence of the Nouri al-Maliki government to seriously work with the Sunni Arab elite, the American imposition of the Baghdad gulag: all these factors dissolve in the deadly daily embrace of the Red Zone—where a human life means absolutely nothing and to stay alive in one piece is a victory to be earned minute by minute.

The Red Zone soundtrack is the hum of the power generator, punctuated by Kalashnikov shots, explosions, bombings, the sirens of police cars and ambulances and the roar of US choppers flying almost at roof level.

The air is heavy, dusty and the sun usually does not shine through the thick haze—a Hollywood-like special effect. The Baghdad gulag has the feel of an eerie version of post-apocalyptic Los Angeles—dusty and dead instead of glitzy palm trees, living-dead characters covered by a thick layer of sand and soot. The urban tissue is of a dissected cadaver—filthy, exposed parts separated from one another, fear and loathing impressed on blood, sweat, tears and viscera.

This is the real face of Bush's surgeland.

ℴ

Baghdad—former Saddam—International Airport is the only airport in the world where immigration does not ask you for your passport: they want your badge. Any foreigner is assumed to be working for the occupation. A passport with a visa provided by the Iraqi Ministry of Foreign Affairs is a certified UFO. Incoming planes still have to circle overhead at least five times before a mad dash towards the runway: one never knows when the Islamic State of Iraq may decide to test drive one of its new al-Quds 1 guided missiles.

The pattern of going round in circles is mirrored on the ground in the taxi ride from the airport via the eerily desolate, coalition-approved ring road to the first checkpoint, bordering the immense, sprawling US Camp Victory nestled behind huge walls and barbed wire. For a foreigner, hanging out at this checkpoint for more than a minute is absolute madness. "It's full of spies," and kidnapping would be a foregone conclusion.

The badge syndrome becomes more apparent in one of the safest places in the Red Zone: it had to be a mini-Green Zone, in the Shiite Karrada neighborhood. A group of no more than 10 houses, including two hotels, is protected like a bunker. Inside this normality amid chaos, the prominent inhabitants had to be armed-to-the-teeth private security contractors—the shadow US army in Iraq. Exit a group of bulky, burly South African mercenaries who had been sipping tea in the hotel lobby over piped music. Enter a group of Nepalese Gurkhas in T-shirts whose first activity is target practice at the hotel entrance.

This Red Zone film set (which would cost a fortune and months of work in Hollywood), "safer than the Green Zone," quips an Iraqi security guard, is the essence of Baghdad gulag territory: blast walls, badges, barbed wire, watchtowers, non-stop security checks, body searches, giant power generators, containers, dilapidated houses (some "for rent," no takers), crumbling pavement, pools of stagnant water.

Security is provided by one of the private companies based in the compound. Baghdad condo living is expensive: power cuts are continual (most of Baghdad has no more than two hours of electricity a day), so energy is at a premium and fuel costs 88 US cents a liter. A medium-sized, three-storey hotel consumes 1,650 liters a day. Sometimes buildings have to run for two or three days on generator only.

Muhammad is a night watchman in this "secure environment." During the day he lives in the real world, in Sadr City, one of the world's foremost slums. He says he faces no problems coming to work every day: after all, he has a badge. He is glad to confirm Muqtada al-Sadr is in Iraq, not Iran, as the White House is claiming. He complains heavily about "Wahabbis killing women and children"—a reference to the Islamic State of Iraq proclaimed by al-Qaeda. And he fears a return of the Ba'athists. For his part, a Christian Kurd head waiter confirms Christians are coming in droves from explosive Dora—where ethnic cleansing by the Islamic State of Iraq is in progress—to live in safety in Karrada: "East Baghdad is safe, but the west is very dangerous. Iraq is finished."

For Kurds and Christians in Karrada, the former Ba'athist, US intelligence asset, interim prime minister and "Butcher of Fallujah," Iyad Allawi, is the closest to a solution to the Iraqi tragedy: "We need a strongman. He would eradicate the militias." They see a weak government and endless party squabbling as the biggest problems—an implicit criticism of the Iran-affiliated religious parties, the Supreme Council for Islam in Iraq (SCII) and the Da'wa Party. They also recognize the split inside the Mahdi Army—and the good nationalist intentions of Muqtada.

Apaches always drown the cry of the muezzin just before sunset. The curfew has been pushed back to 10:00 pm. But even by 5 pm the streets are already deserted. Cultural life is non-existent. The artisans in the souk al-Rashid are gone. The booksellers on al-Mutanabi are gone. The windows in countless buildings remain smashed. The al-Rashid telephone exchange, or the Ministry of Finance, or the Ministry of Planning by the Green Zone, remain post-modern cement deconstructions, Swiss cheese-style.

On Saadoon Street, once one of the main roads, most businesses are closed. Saadoon though exhibits a prime Baghdad contribution to post-modern art, worthy of a Venice Biennale: the landscaped blast wall, featuring colorful scenes of lakeside, mountain or pastoral bliss. The wall, of course, serves the pedestrian purpose of protecting the infamous Baghdad Hotel, a well-known headquarters of US security forces.

In Mansur—former abode of the Baghdad grand bourgeoisie—streets are also blocked by checkpoints and a few houses harboring politicians or businessmen are enveloped by blast walls. The restaurants on Mansur Avenue are all closed. The whole neighborhood also fits the pattern of a film set in ruins. It's impossible to eat a *masgouf*—grilled carp—by the Tigris, on Abu Nawas Street, a former favorite Baghdad pastime: the restaurants are all closed. Saydia used to be a good, relatively upscale Baghdad neighborhood, ethnically mixed, with lots of Ba'ath Party officials but also average civilians. Most houses are now abandoned, the streets empty, only a few stores open.

There may not be as many SUVs with tinted windows whose occupants distribute Kalashnikov rounds at random—or as many car bombs in markets. But the overwhelming majority of Baghdadis, Sunni or Shiite, have absolutely no trust in the capacity of the Maliki government to minimally assure their security.

Abdul Samad Sultan, minister of migrations, insists that over 1,000 self-exiled families have returned to their neighborhoods, mostly in Madaen, Mahmoudiya and Shaab. But that's nothing compared to figures in a recent report by the non-governmental organization International Medical Corps, according to which 540,000 Iraqis had fled their homes from the February 2006 bombing of the Askariya Shrine in Samarra to early 2007. Eighty percent of these—as I had easily confirmed in Damascus—are from Baghdad.

Every Sunni I talk to accuses the Mahdi Army of chasing them out of formerly mixed neighborhoods, while in Yarmouk hardcore Sunnis of the

Islamic Party are advancing their ethnic cleansing of Shiites. Until recently, a gruesome ritual was being performed in Yarmouk—the showing off of the cadavers of the day at noon, or guerrillas telling families to look for their relatives as if they were in Bala, a well-known second-hand market ("you look inside the bags, and you can match an arm with another, or a leg with a foot").

In explosive al-Amriya, in west Baghdad, flags of the Islamic State of Iraq are on full display, and the writing is—literally—on the walls: "Long live al-Qaeda." I can't even think of leaving the Toyota to explore the neighborhood. Women are being forced to wear the *niqqab*—which covers the whole face—and gloves at all times, and some women have already been executed, accused of spying. All across town war widows—women who traditionally were supposed to stay at home raising the family—now have become mechanics, parking valets or electronic appliance repairers.

Sunni Heitein and mixed Sunni-Shiite al-Ameel are adjacent neighborhoods. The ethnic cleansing of Ameel has been persistent for the past four months. It all started—as almost everything in Iraq—as a tribal conflict, between the Sunni al-Janabi tribe and the Shiite al-Megasis tribe. Fighting with Kalashnikovs, mortars and rocket-propelled grenades would go on all day, even during the Friday *jumma* prayers. In the end, Sunnis were forced to leave Ameel for good. The neighborhood became a ghost town, now virtually sealed off by the Iraqi Army.

Iraq's per capita annual income plunged from US$3,600 in 1980—when Iraq was still a model developing country—to US$860 in 2001 after 10 years of United Nations sanctions, to US$530 at the end of 2003. Now it may be even lower than US$400. Unemployment is at 60%. Thieves are desperate: there are not many more flush Iraqis left to plunder. The only lucrative business is to kidnap and resell foreigners. Thus the desperation of Abdel and Fatima as I insist on crisscrossing the town.

As I have seen in Damascus, an extremely high percentage of Iraqi exiles are businessmen, technocrats, intellectuals, scientists—all fleeing fundamentalist or confessional carnage, whether it comes from militias, death squads, mafias, killers disguised as policemen, Saddamists or Salafi-jihadists. The absence of skilled workers and professionals in Baghdad is absolutely staggering. A well-known secular intellectual, whose identity also must be protected, has been insistently courted by the Maliki government: they have offered anything he wanted, even a ministry. He declined. The Sunni Arab resistance also offered him anything he wanted. He also declined. No one knows how much longer he can maintain his independence.

Most of the five million or so poor souls who have remained in Baghdad are the disenfranchised, the unemployed, the miserable, the wretched, like scores of old, frail men in their battered *gallabie* and *keffiah* begging in the middle of the hellish traffic, among the decomposing cars, the donkeys, the slaughtered sheep by the curbside and the endless machine gun toting convoys of Iraqi police ("They are worse than the Americans").

The UN has done next to nothing to help these millions of exiled Iraqis—not to mention the wealthy Arab emirates, or the Wahhabi millionaires in Saudi Arabia. After the total implosion of social life, Iraq has reverted to pre-modernity. Baghdad, once the pride of Islam, has reverted to the status of the saddest, most desperate of global capitals. No wonder the motto—even from secular, well-educated Shiites—is ubiquitous: "Iraq is finished."

So no one can say that half a trillion dollars—so far—courtesy of US taxpayers, has not served a clear "creative destruction" purpose. And this is only the hors d'oeuvres. The Baghdad gulag is yet to reach full fruition. Iraq will be finished one mini-Green Zone at a time.

7: An inflation of dead al-Qaedas

The breaking news comes around noon, on state-run Al-Iraqiya TV, and hits Sadr City, as well as the rest of Baghdad, as a new "shock and awe": Sheikh Abu Hamza al-Muhajir, popularly known in Baghdad as Abu al-Masri, the Egyptian-born leader of al-Qaeda in Iraq, had been killed in the al-Nabai area of Taji, north Baghdad. That's what Interior Ministry spokesman Brigadier-General Abu al-Kareem Khalaf was telling Al-Iraqiya live—to the incredulity of many a viewer.

But the spokesman was also saying something even more striking. Abu al-Masri had not been killed by militias at the ministry (the seventh floor is considered "Iranian territory"; virtually no one is admitted). He had not been killed by death squads. And he had not been killed by US forces. He fell victim to "internal fighting"—which could be a reference to a coalition of Sunni tribes that has been fighting al-Qaeda's extreme methods, or even to al-Qaeda itself. Khalaf actually said Masri was killed by his own al-Qaeda jihadis in an ambush at the Safi Bridge north of Baghdad, an assertion that had to be taken with an extreme pinch of salt.

The reaction in almost-3-million-strong Sadr City—where al-Qaeda in Iraq (or "the Wahhabis") is viewed as worse than any plague—was predictably ecstatic. There was jubilation at police checkpoints (all of them manned by al-Sadr's Mahdi Army). But then came the "ifs"—Masri's death had already been officially announced twice in the past few months. The ministry had "definitive intelligence reports" Masri was dead. But it had not seen the corpse yet. The Pentagon could not confirm anything.

Then government spokesman Ali al-Dabbagh showed up, once again on Al-Iraqiya, saying, "This does not represent an official government announcement." The truth would only emerge after a series of DNA tests. If, of course, there was a body. Interior Ministry officials would only say, "Our people have seen the body."

Finally, inevitably, came the denials. The Islamic State of Iraq hit the internet with a vengeance, proclaiming to the *ummah*, "Sheikh Abu Hamza al-Mujahir, God protect him, is alive and he is still fighting the enemy of God."

So what, in fact, was really happening?

Masri had been the leader of al-Qaeda in Iraq—personally approved by Osama bin Laden—since June 2006, when former uber-bogeyman Abu Musab al-Zarqawi was killed by a US air strike in Diyala. Like Ayman al-Zawahiri, al-Qaeda's No. 2, he is a former member of the Egyptian Islamic Jihad. In November 2006, al-Qaeda in Iraq announced the formation of the Islamic State of Iraq, a Salafi-jihadist constellation. Masri was the new state's "minister of war." The leader of the Islamic State of Iraq is Abu Omar al-Baghdadi.

Al-Qaeda in Iraq has been striving to impose the fierce Salafi-jihadist Wahhabi ethos and consolidate hegemonic power among the myriad groups in the Sunni Arab resistance. Most of these groups are patriotic and nationalist, and many are crammed with ex-Ba'athists: naturally they view foreign "Wahhabis" with extreme suspicion.

So a backlash was inevitable. In the autumn of 2006, more than two hundred powerful Sunni sheikhs in al-Anbar province constituted the Anbar Sovereignty Council—led by powerful Sheikh Abd al-Sattar Abu Risha—basically to counteract al-Qaeda in Iraq.

According to council rules, every family in Anbar province must give at least one son to the struggle. By the spring of 2007, nine key Sunni Arab resistance groups—including Jaysh Ansar al-Sunnah, the Islamic Front for the Iraqi Resistance, and the fierce al-Qaeda in Iraq enemy, the 1920 Revolution Brigades—issued a statement positioning themselves against the US occupation, against Prime Minister Nouri al-Maliki's government and against the Islamic State of Iraq and its leader, Baghdadi.

Baghdadi may have boasted that Iraq, under US occupation, has been turned into "a university for jihad." But the fact is the Islamic State of Iraq was being besieged by US and Iraqi forces in Baquba. There was a lot of nuance, though. According to Pentagon spin, what was happening in Anbar was a battle of US counterinsurgency versus al-Qaeda. Wrong: what was really happening was the Islamic State of Iraq/ al-Qaeda in Iraq against the non-Salafi-jihadist Sunni Arab resistance. The 1920 Revolutionary Brigades and Ansar al-Sunnah had been attacking al-Qaeda in Iraq almost daily in Diyala, Salahuddin and Anbar. The key issue was the split between al-Qaeda and former Ba'athists—a split that has always been fierce.

Whether true or not, we already knew from the start the killing of Masri would make absolutely no difference—as did the killing of Zarqawi. The Islamic State of Iraq's tentacles are so far-reaching they have already deeply infiltrated Baghdad neighborhoods such as Amriya and Dora. One, two, a thousand Masris are waiting in the wings. Al-Qaeda's strategy won't change—and that means non-stop bloody bombings to keep inciting Sunnis to attack the majority Shiites.

The so-called "sanctions generation" in Iraq—those who grew up under the dreaded United Nations sanctions during the 1990s—will keep churning out legions of ready-to-die martyrs. And most of all, hardcore Islamists—local and foreign—as well as Arab nationalists will continue to fight a common enemy: the US occupation.

8: The "savior"

He is a former Sunni Arab mujahid from Ramadi who until recently was fighting the US occupation. He has only a secondary education and is married with two wives. Now he is praised even by urban, secular, highly educated Shiites as a "conscious man," or "the kind of man we need now in Iraq." Sheikh Abdul Satter Abu Risha is the leader of the Anbar Sovereignty Council, a powerful coalition of Anbar tribes, including at least 200 sheikhs, that is fighting the Salafi jihadis of al-Qaeda in Iraq/the Islamic Emirate of Iraq in the ultra-volatile province.

Abu Risha set up the council after his father and two brothers were killed by al-Qaeda's extreme methods in the autumn of 2006. I could not possibly travel unescorted to Ramadi to meet him: Abdel and Fatima told me it would be suicide. In a telephone interview the Sheikh stated, unambiguously, that al-Qaeda "has abused our traditions and generosity" and, he alleged, they even "take drugs"—a mortal sin in conservative Islam.

Sheikh Ali Hattan al-Suleiman, also from the council, was even more direct: "I'd like to see an al-Qaeda bomber e-mail me or telephone me and talk about his education. They just came here with money. They gave money to the unemployed. They are not Iraqis—only Arabs. They are bastards. And the people who follow them are also bastards."

Abu Risha totally dismissed rumors that the Anbar council is forcing families in the region to give their sons to the cause, or is engaged in summary execution of captured jihadis. "We only accept volunteers. And we work by ourselves, like a team, by shifts. When we arrest people from al-Qaeda or Iraqis working for al-Qaeda, we take them to the Iraqi Army or the Ministry of Interior."

It was fair to assume, though, that once these jihadis end up in the hands of the ministry's death squads, torture and death are inevitable. Resistance to capture also means jihadis are killed on the spot. And when the going gets really rough, "sometimes we call for American air strikes."

With young, disfranchised Iraqis who have been seduced by al-Qaeda's rhetoric and financial muscle, it's a different story. "When we capture these teenagers, we try to convince them they were wrong, they just were seduced by money, and we try to give them back to their families."

The Sunni Arab resistance in Iraq is at least 100,000-strong. Salafi- jihadis, mostly foreigners—from Saudi Arabia, Kuwait, Egypt, Palestine, North Africa, and a few "white Moors" (European Muslims)—may be no more than 1,000. Only a small percentage of these are Iraqi recruits.

Abu Risha swore that the Iraqi Army and US forces were now controlling Ramadi. Fallujah is a very different story—according to Sunni Iraqi journalists who had been to the front line. They told me the outskirts of west Baghdad are safe up to Abu Ghraib, but not Fallujah, which has been an Islamic State of Iraq stronghold. According to the Sheikh, al-Qaeda in Iraq is particularly active in al-Rahwa (a big city near the Syrian border), Tilal Himrin (a village also near Syria), the village of Elbu Baly, and the big city of Balad.

Prime Minister Nouri al-Maliki had promised more than US$100 million for rebuilding Ramadi in 2007. Abu Risha said, without elaborating, that "support from the government has not been enough," whether financially or militarily. It was well known in Baghdad that the Sheikh had been traveling to Syria and Jordan to rally Sunni tribes to the council's cause— and he added, "The borders with Syria and Jordan are all patrolled by our forces," implying the difficulty for jihadis to cross over.

Abu Risha insisted he gets active cooperation "from all tribes"—and that includes border surveillance. The fact is, 80% of these tribes are sub-clans of the powerful al-Dulaimi tribe. Instead, al-Qaeda's close relationship is with the al-Mashadani, a big tribe very much present near Samarra and Balad. The Mashadani tribe detests the Maliki government, and the Ibrahim Jaafari government before it. They used to be very close to Saddam Hussein. Now, they have an alliance of circumstance with al-Qaeda.

Abu Risha certainly has political aspirations. "If the government is weak, they should move aside and leave space for other, prepared people." The Sheikh wants to set up a tribal political coalition, which would be called "Revival of the Sheikhs of Iraq." Now the Anbar Sovereignty Council has even changed its name to "Iraq Awakening." It plans to take government matters into its own hands, and distribute food rations to the population of Anbar province.

The relentless info war in Iraq degenerates virtually every day into total confusion. For example, after this talk with Abu Risha, the whole thing unraveled once again. Two days after breaking the news of the killing of al-Qaeda in Iraq leader Abu al-Masri—which in the end turned out to be false—state-run Al-Iraqiyah TV broke the news of the killing of none other than Abu Omar al-Baghdadi, the leader of the Islamic State of Iraq, which includes al-Qaeda. The greenish photo of a very bloated face in an open coffin, with visible specks of blood, was splashed all over Iraq's newspapers.

Interior Ministry spokesman Brigadier Abdul Karim Khalaf once again was sure: this was Abu Omar al-Baghdadi, and he had been killed in west Baghdad, in Ghazaliya, which had been controlled by the Sunni Arab resistance for quite a long time. Later, information circulated that his body had been handed over to his own tribe—and they were already setting up a huge funeral street tent in their home town, Duluiyah, between Baghdad and Samarra, as is custom in Iraq.

Was it Baghdadi? Well, maybe not. It was for the Supreme Council for Islam in Iraq (SCII) and the SCII-controlled Ministry of Interior—and apparently for no one else. The Interior Ministry maintained that the corpse was recognized by residents of Duluiyah as Abu Omar al-Baghdadi. The Pentagon, once again, would not confirm anything. Instead, the Americans announced that "Masri"—who might have died two days before—was in fact al-Qaeda in Iraq's minister of information, Abdel Latif al-Jubouri, his identity confirmed by DNA tests and photos. His corpse was then handed to his tribe. Masri as well as Baghdadi still seemed to be alive.

39

Interestingly enough, Abu Risha had also been "sure" that Masri was dead. Initial reports attributed Masri's killing to Abu Risha's forces. Then the Pentagon claimed it was US forces who actually killed Jubouri. To add to the inextricable mess, Iraqi Interior and Defense Ministry officials started spreading the news that Jubouri and Baghdadi were the same person. The fact is that regarding the shadowy world of al-Qaeda in Iraq nobody, absolutely nobody knows anything for sure.

What people did know and had started to notice was the increasingly high profile of Sheikh Abu Risha. He may not be Iraq's savior, but as the larger-than-life tragedy of Iraq stands, a Sunni Sheikh leading a tribal coalition fighting alongside a predominantly Shiite Iraqi government against Salafi-jihadist terror was better news than any "international community" rhetorical flourishes emanating from innocuous Middle East summits.

9: Leave now or we will behead you

The message comes in the dead of night, a scrawled piece of paper slipped under the door: "If you don't leave, we will behead you." This is what remaining Iraqi Christians face and fear in Dora, Baghdad's vortex of ethnic and confessional cleansing. Terrified residents, who insist on their anonymity, paint a picture of hell worthy of Hieronymus Bosch: "The good have all gone; only the savages remain."

Dora is a middle-class neighborhood by the Tigris, predominantly Sunni, in southwest Baghdad. It's a collection of small farms, groves, orchards and fruit gardens in essence peopled by two large tribes—al-Dulaimi and al-Jobouri. The groves extend all the way to Madan, and connect to other Baghdad neighborhoods. Some very comfortable houses—property of local sheikhs—are located in these farms. Saddam Hussein himself once had a house in Dora.

Dora is thus a perfect setting for the *muqawama*—the Sunni Arab resistance, as it is referred to by most Iraqis—to thrive; in Mao Zedong's terms, the "sea" where the "fish" thrive. Residents identify the favorite guerrilla regions as the Elbu area, where "Shiites have always been killed," Hura and Arab al-Jubour. So not only Christians are victims: according to non-official numbers, by the spring of 2007 no fewer than 1,682 Shiites had been killed in Dora since 2003—most of them on their pilgrimage to Karbala—and 894 have been kidnapped (and most subsequently killed).

During the months in 2002 when he was preparing for the real war in Iraq—after the inevitable US invasion—Saddam sent countless messengers to farmers in areas like Dora, and bought small plots of land everywhere. Then, in the middle of the night, Revolutionary Guards would come and bury loads of weapons and cash for the future resistance.

But Dora also became a haven for al-Qaeda in Iraq. Former bogeyman Abu Musab al-Zarqawi, residents told me, was always lurking in Dora. Sheikh Abu Risha—the leader of the Anbar Sovereignty Council who is fighting al-Qaeda in Iraq in the province—had already expelled them from Ramadi once, and also after the American assault on Fallujah in late 2004. Their preferred destination was Dora.

This all ties with Saddam's policies since he climbed to power in 1979. He expelled virtually all Shiites from west Baghdad. In the arc from north to west and southwest around Baghdad, there are only Sunnis. This has assured ample support for the Saddamist front in the resistance, and has also assured a "Sunni corridor" for the mobile, ever-morphing Salafi-jihadis.

The Salafi-jihadist front itself, always morphing, by the spring of 2007 comprised three main currents. There's the Sururiyyah movement, which is a cocktail of Salafi Muslim Brotherhood fighters. There's the Islamic Front of the Iraqi Resistance—which is basically Hamas in Iraq. And there's the Islamic State of Iraq, which contains al-Qaeda in Iraq. The latter is responsible for the terror in Dora.

Residents identified a key terror figure as one Najra, a son of one of the Dora sheikhs—a former Ba'athist who has pledged his allegiance to al-Qaeda in Iraq. But the top man may be Sheikh Tahan al-Jubouri, who is very close to Abu al-Masri, the leader of al-Qaeda in Iraq who had been reported killed (unconfirmed) by the Iraqi government.

A Dora resident says, "Everyone here can be a victim of random shootings; they attack people in the markets, or people walking in the streets." A middle-class Sunni woman—with a Shiite husband—living in her own family's house, not her husband's, tells how her husband was attacked right in front of the house. Not only was he killed, she was forced to leave and now has resettled in another Baghdad neighborhood.

At the last count, in 1977—before even the Iran-Iraq War—1,684,000 Christians were living unmolested in Iraq. After the first Gulf War of 1991, 12 years of United Nations sanctions and the 2003 "shock and awe," all that is known is that the remaining majority still lived in the neighborhoods of

Dora and New Baghdad, including the 6,000 families who live near a church in Dora.

Residents remember the horror stories started toward the end of 2004—about the time of the assault on Fallujah—with attacks on five big churches plus another one in Mosul, which is considered by many in Iraq to be the first church ever built in the world. Iraqi governments tend to play down the confessional cleansing: by the spring of 2007, according to official numbers, of 122 Christians assassinated since the US invasion in 2003, only 18 had been certified in Baghdad.

Yet since late 2005, "a lot of people" have left, according to residents. "Now there is no market, no vegetables, no bakeries, everything is closed." Indeed it is. During the day Dora is an eerie, ghostly shadow of its former garden incarnation. There's absolutely no chance of seeing an unveiled woman in the streets on the way to buy groceries; if that's the case, one resident says, kids riding bicycles force her to wear the *hijab*.

Members of a well-to-do family tell how they received the infamous "letter under the door." The whole family left Dora for Shiite Kadhimiya—site of a revered shrine—and left the house empty; it has been noted by "scouts," and is now probably occupied by Salafi-jihadis. Now they share a house with other families, paying the astronomical rent of 1 million dinars (almost US$ 10,000) a month. Mizar Yalda, a 48-year-old priest, says that according to his calculations, 190 Dora residents have been kidnapped since the 2003 invasion, and have paid a collective ransom of more than US$ 480,000.

If you are a Christian and you want to keep living in Dora, you must convert to Islam. Not only that, you must also cooperate with al-Qaeda in Iraq, and must accept al-Qaeda refugees into your house when they are trying to escape hot pursuit. If you refuse, you will be killed.

By some perverted math, al-Qaeda in Iraq has established that if you don't want to convert, you must pay US$1,600 per person—plus the assurance that you won't denounce anything concerning al-Qaeda in Iraq's activities. Residents confirm that "some people paid" and are still in Dora. But "some converted"; recently there had been talk of 24 men, six women and three girls who did so. What is certain is that the majority of Christians have left. Amel Zaya paid US$7,600 to Jobouri to stay in Dora with her family, and also for "protection." She now runs a restaurant.

So how does the US occupation army react to all this madness? The bombastic way. Less than two weeks before I got in touch with Dora's residents, the Buaitha area of Dora was subjected to an artillery barrage and no fewer than 24 explosions from US Base Falcon—in broad daylight. There's no evidence that al-Qaeda in Iraq has been debilitated by this "tactic"—not exactly the subtlest way to fight confessional cleansing and win hearts and minds.

10: Back to "Saddam without a mustache"

From secular, well-educated Shiites to in-love-with-the-West Kurds, from Christians suffering ethnic cleansing to even some moderate Sunnis, Iraqis terrified by the current carnage are more and more inclined to turn to Iyad Allawi as the only possible solution. "We need a strongman," says Hamoodi, a young Kurd from Sulaymaniah who got his visa approved and will continue his medicine studies in Michigan in the US; he does not plan on coming back. There's a virtual consensus among people in Baghdad that security under Allawi's interim premiership was relatively OK, deteriorated under Ibrahim al-Jaafari and reached nightmarish levels under Nouri al-Maliki.

Iyad Allawi used to be referred to in Baghdad as "Saddam without a mustache." The ex-Ba'athist, embezzler-in-Yemen and former CIA and MI5 asset also became "the butcher of Fallujah" after ordering the massive assault on the Sunni belt resistance stronghold in November 2004. Not to mention his push against Muqtada al-Sadr's followers in Najaf, also in 2004. But the civil war has enhanced his popular perception as non-sectarian. The true measure of the overwhelming Iraqi tragedy is that people in Baghdad are now yearning for an ersatz Saddam.

By the spring of 2007 there were insistent rumors in Baghdad of a US-inspired "white coup" in Parliament to finish off with Maliki's ineffective government and install Allawi as the new Prime Minister. For this end Allawi was even talking to the Sadrists. Ibtisan al-Awadi, a former member of Parliament for the Iraqi List, which has four ministers, was the negotiator in charge.

The development was quite surprising, considering the extremely strained relationship between Allawi and Muqtada because of the attack on Najaf. But the fact is nobody—except for SCII and Da'wa—seems to be supporting Maliki. Popular perception in Baghdad among educated urban Shiites also rules that politicians from Da'wa are generally well educated, but those from SCII are mostly appalling.

Azat al-Shabander is Allawi's spokesman. He told me "we have good relations with all the political parties against the government. There is also a great deal of armed groups who have abandoned their weapons and prefer peace. We are in favor of no loyalty to Iran. This is the big difference between us and the governments of Jaafari and Maliki."

As things stand, Shabander likes to emphasize that "the US supports Maliki. Bush has said it many times. This is clear." But Shabander also makes a point that "the US did not privilege anybody during these four years, nor interfered." What would make Allawi a better prime minister than Maliki? "He is known as the director of a national, and not confessional, project. This puts him in a very comfortable position."

Allawi, says Shabander, "strongly condemns the Shiite political parties who suffer interference from Iran. True Iraqi Shiites don't accept this intervention." He says Allawi has "good relations" with Saudi Arabia although always vigilant, because "sometimes they support religious parties here with a lot of money"—an oblique reference to wahhabi support for the Sunni Arab resistance. Allawi has been to Saudi Arabia building alliances—unlike Maliki, who was famously snubbed by King Abdullah. He travels as much as most Iraqi politicians—who spend most of their time in Cairo, Amman, Damascus or, for that matter, London. Not bad for a hefty US$15,000 a month salary. During the 2007 Eid festivities, members of Parliament got "gifts" to the tune of almost US$60,000 each.

Shabander sounds like an Israeli politician when he argues Allawi's point for defending the Adhamiyah wall: "This is not a wall; it's a partition barrier that the security forces find useful for controlling who enters and who exits a dangerous zone. It's not an isolated wall. People who are against the wall are just blowing it out of proportion." This "against the wall" crowd happens to include the population of Adhamiyah itself.

Shabander stresses that Allawi "hopes the US establishes good relations with all other countries in the region to the benefit of Iraq"—a message that obviously concerns US-Iran relations. A new non-sectarian coalition may be emerging in Iraq—against the current Shiite/Kurd majority government, and that coalition might be led by Allawi. As Shabander never tires to point out, "we have cooperation with all national groups." But a government of Iraqi national unity is still just a dream. "Saddam without a mustache" is convinced he's the right man for the intractable job. So is Washington.

11: The Mahdi against the Dajjal

Despite being on the receiving end of waves and waves of demonization in the US, Muqtada al-Sadr is, hands down, the most popular, and certainly the most charismatic, political leader in Iraq, with his ears finely tuned to the Shiite—and even Sunni—street.

Nasr al-Roubaie is the leader of the 32-strong Sadrist bloc in the Iraqi Parliament. As Muqtada's top man in government, Roubaie could not but be one of Iraq's top political players. Between two crucial parliamentary meetings, Roubaie took time to talk to me—symbolically on the outer limits of the Green Zone, practically in the Red Zone itself, outside the first checkpoint, manned by Georgian troops who speak virtually no English and absolutely no Arabic. The Sadrists, we should remember, are—literally—both inside and outside the Green Zone government.

The Sadr movement is an absolute magnet to deprived southern Shiites—via its ample provision of social services. That's exactly what Muqtada's father used to do. As for the Mahdi Army, created by Muqtada in the summer of 2003, it was never instructed to attack the American occupation, like the Sunni Arab *muqawama*. It was a defensive force, which only radicalized when the Sadrists were directly attacked by the Americans in 2004.

Roubaie emphasized to me the key Sadrist strategy that a timetable must be set for the total withdrawal of US troops—and Madam Speaker Nancy Pelosi as well as 64% of American voters, according to spring of 2007 polls, would certainly agree. "Our fight has developed in many different ways. Some are peaceful. Some are armed. We are engaged in political resistance. We want to get our real freedom through peaceful means," Roubaie told me.

So far, peace between the Baghdad surge and Muqtada's Mahdi Army had been a mirage—even considering the fact that the Mahdi Army, on Muqtada's explicit orders, had been lying very low. I spoke to Roubaie the day after US forces attacked the Sadr office in Kadhimiya—which houses a very holy Shiite shrine. Residents confirmed a heavy firefight. Two US Humvees were burned, and nine Iraqi civilians were killed. A large street demonstration took place in Kadhimiya. The result was that US forces now can get no closer than 1 km to any important Shiite shrine.

Roubaie had just come from a meeting where a motion signed by 134 Iraqi Parliament members was being introduced demanding a timetable for US withdrawal. "It's not only us—the parties from Kurdistan, the Sunni parties, are all united." This was a reference to the Kurdistan alliance and the powerful, 44-seat-strong Tawafuq Front Sunni bloc, which groups three parties. Roubaie left implicit that the key religious parties in government, the Supreme Council for Islam in Iraq (SCII) and Da'wa, were against the timetable.

Every year the Iraqi Parliament reviews the presence of US occupation forces. Roubaie revealed that starting in June 2007, the review would take place every six months. "The Americans want to stay in Iraq. They said they wanted to establish an Iraqi force. They did nothing—we still have no army. And they did nothing for the people."

In a letter to Parliament, read by Sadrist female member Liqa' al-Yassin, Muqtada characterized the Iraq drama as a fight between the Mahdi against the Dajjal, an evil, one-eyed entity similar to the antichrist in Shiite cosmology. George W. Bush, of course, is the Dajjal. Muqtada also emphasized that Bush "ignores every call for a withdrawal."

So if the Americans want to stay, this has to be connected with oil, and the extremely controversial new Iraqi oil law, which should, in theory, be approved by Parliament during the summer of 2007 (at least according to the explicit "benchmarks" set by the Bush administration). Roubaie said, "The oil of Iraq should benefit all of our people. We cannot hand out our oil wells to foreign companies with these production-sharing agreements. The sovereignty of Iraq will be compromised. This will be only pen on paper, like the last orders of the Abbasid caliphs. Our oil wells should benefit all Iraqis."

The Sadrists want an oil law that "is the symbol of the unity of Iraq, and not good only for the Kurds or for the south." Here we find the Sadrists in essence concurring with Saddam Hussein, who nationalized the Iraqi oil industry in 1972.

Once again the criticism of the top government parties, the SCIII and Da'wa, is implicit. Abdul Adel Mahdi, the SCII's No 2, has been one of the top cheerleaders of the oil law; he has been to Washington to assure Big Oil of the "great opportunities" lying ahead. Oil Minister Husain al-Shahrastani, from Da'wa, is also a top cheerleader, arguing that the oil law "will benefit all Iraqis" and boasting that the country may raise oil production to 4 million barrels a day until 2012, and then to 8 million barrels a day. According to the minister, Iraq currently exports 2.2 million barrels a day—a very dubious figure considering non-stop pipeline sabotage by Sunni guerrillas.

By the spring of 2007 there was a real possibility in the months ahead of an Iraqi shadow cabinet being formed—uniting Sadrists and Sunni nationalists. This posed the striking alternative confronting Iraq's government: What would prevail, Iraqi nationalism—as represented by Muqtada—or a semi-alignment with Iran—represented by the SCII and Da'wa? As for Muqtada, he would always remain the kingmaker.

"Is he in Iran or Iraq?" I asked, before Roubaie re-entered the Green Zone. "Of course in Iraq," he answered with a huge grin, as a column of US Bradleys rumbled back to its cozy abode in the Green Zone. So the White House, once again, had been spinning a lie about Muqtada, an Iraqi nationalist, having fled the country to take refuge "among the Persians."

12: Inside Sadr City

This is the (under)privileged 24 square km theatre where a great part of Iraq's future is being played; a vital element in Bush's surge; the place Pentagon generals dream of smashing into submission; one of the largest slums in the world, and arguably the most notorious.

Sadr (former Saddam) City is also, along with Gaza and the West Bank, the privileged theatre of the already evolving 21st century war, pitting the high-tech Western haves against the slum-dwelling Third World have-nots. If the Bush administration had any intention of conquering any hearts and minds in Iraq, this is where it would be trying the hardest. Reality spells otherwise.

Sadr City is an immense grid in eastern Baghdad of ramshackle one-storey buildings covered with dust—not unlike slums in northern Africa or Pakistan. The main streets like boulevard Gouarder are lined with Iraqi, not partisan, flags. A few black flags denote houses of descendents of Prophet Muhammad's family. There are photos of late Ayatollah Muhammad Baqr al-Sadr—killed by Saddam's goons—even in billboards advertising mobile phones. Muqtada al-Sadr's office is a modest building near the main crossroads—not far from the street market which was hit by a horrific bombing in January 2007 that killed 250 people and wounded more than 400. There are plenty of sidewalk funeral tents—as is the custom in Iraq. Sadr City residents who fall victim to the carnage in Baghdad can be counted by the dozens on certain days.

Vans or pickup trucks carrying coffins pass by (in other parts of Baghdad, usually in the morning, pickup trucks carrying bodies or body parts pass by, severed legs and hands dangling, sometimes falling on the pavement). The radio station of choice is Peace 106 FM. Kids in Argentine soccer jerseys play in the streets alongside women in full chador (no chance of seeing any woman unveiled). Gasoline in the black market—promoted by kids by the curbside waving plastic containers—is extremely expensive: 80 US cents a liter. But there is no shortage of battered collective vehicles in the streets; the local buses look like rolling cadavers.

People have only one hour of electricity every six hours; sometimes nothing, for two or three days. The absolute majority cannot afford big generators (one ampere costs 9000 dinars, almost US$8). So the answer is the cheap made in Korea Astra portable fuel generator, selling for US$200 a piece. There is no phone service; virtually everybody carries a mobile phone.

Hussein al-Motery is the general administrator of the municipality of Sadr City, the man ultimately responsible for the wellbeing of almost 3 million people, more than half the current population of Baghdad. Every day, after sunset prayers, rows of people come to his modest house to ask for favors or jobs ("I'm always in contact with the people"). Unemployment in Iraq is usually estimated at a whopping 60%; Hussein has no figures, but in Sadr City it may be even higher ("Even people with university degrees have no jobs"). Hussein admits "I was lucky, I graduated, I have the chance to own a house." Eleven people per house—usually sleeping in the same room—is a fact of life all over Sadr City.

Sadr City is a giant dormitory. Hussein says "Baghdad would become a ghost city if people from Sadr City would not go there to work." He adds that "Sadr City has become the symbol of stability for Baghdad and Iraq. Many merchants in Baghdad come from Sadr City." Community life is indeed stable; this is a peaceful, harmonious dormitory (Hussein describes local people as "naïve, they accept everything, they have a great sense of sacrifice"). Residents confirm they feel secure inside Sadr City, but never outside. They are not in the habit of complaining; a common expression is *Sali ala al Nabi* ("Pray for the Prophet"), meaning in the end everything will be alright.

Take Hussein Maheidel, from Amara in Shiite southern Iraq, who's been living in Sadr City for the past 30 years. He was a construction worker, but has been handicapped for the past 12 years because of a nerve problem in his back. All the best Iraqi doctors have left the country; so an operation might not be successful. He has no pension to support his family of nine children. So he's being helped by the office of Muqtada al-Sadr, who pays his monthly rent of US$ 100, a figure considered low in Sadr City. The average monthly rental for a house in the neighborhood is US$ 750.

The Maheidel family lives in bleak poverty and sleeps in the same small room. But the head of the household is not complaining. He hopes his children "will not be workers, like myself." They are all in school; the unfortunate exception is his 6-year-old daughter, who spends the day caring for his father (he walks on crutches). The expression of infinite sadness in her eyes is extremely disturbing. There are polite smiles in Sadr City—but the impression is they are directed to the lone foreign visitor. Resignation in sadness is the feeling among most adults.

Maheidel believes Muqtada "is a good leader." He says "the Americans came to our house at night, walking, they didn't search the house, but they were ready to attack." Security in his district is provided by tribal guards, and not by Muqtada al-Sadr's Mahdi Army. Everyone in the district seems to agree Sadr City is the most peaceful place in Iraq. The heavy turbulence is another story—it involves the deadly clashes between the Mahdi Army against the Americans, Sunni guerrillas or al- Qaeda in Iraq.

Hussein tries somewhat to be lenient with the Maliki government: "The problem is Parliament did not allot money for Sadr City according to our necessities." Because of its reputation as a safe neighborhood, Hussein says a lot of people from other parts of Iraq are moving into Sadr City. Each district has two schools. Sheikh Ali Hasan, very elegant in his brown robe, responsible for one of Sadr City's districts, says there are over 100 schools in the neighborhood, but as Hussein points out, "the number of students exceeds the places we have available." There are plans to build a local university. The municipality already has the land, 300 hectares; they also want to build a medical center and a park. But they need help. And no help is coming from the Maliki government. As Hussein points out, "anyone successful, or responsible, Maliki, Allawi, would have to do something for us."

According to Hussein and Sheikh Hasan, there are also not enough health services in Sadr City. Caring for almost 3 million people, there are only two general hospitals (one of them for children), one woman's hospital and a few clinics. "Our doctors have united and have taken some initiatives. But we lack everything. Especially with this government, they are not stable."

Hussein remembers how "after the fall of Saddam, there were a lot of good expectations. But the Americans came here with no architects or machines. They think they have the right to do anything they want." He refers to the recent one-million-men-march from Kufa to Najaf called by Muqtada al-Sadr: "If the Americans had any sensibility, they would have left Iraq."

Hussein and Sheikh Hasan confirm the Americans always "come at night, sometimes by day, always protected by helicopters." They "sometimes bomb houses, sometimes arrest people, sometimes throw missiles." Three months ago "they surrounded Sadr City. They keep doing it sometimes, for a few hours." Hussein is adamant: "This is not a dangerous place. You can walk around anywhere. Even Sunnis live here. Our director of Finance, he lives in Adhamiyah, he comes to work here. Many women officials too. The other way around, it would not be possible."

It's been a long time since Muqtada al-Sadr himself has been to Sadr City. Every resident says something to the effect that "he is in our hearts." Hussein stresses "I am an Iraqi first, but also a Sadrist. Muqtada is always with us. We even listen to his whispers. He is the only musician in our country, the orchestra is playing other things. He is the only leader who has called for the unity of Iraq."

Muqtada's speech where he accused Bush of building "non-national and non-Islamic walls of political and sectarian division" struck an extremely powerful chord in Sadr City. Were the Pentagon tempted to wall

Sadr City, the feeling is that nearly 3 million people would instantly be up in arms. There had been rumors that Muqtada had directed the Mahdi Army to attack any trucks in Baghdad transporting concrete blocks. But no one in Sadr City would confirm it.

Even urban, highly educated, secular Shiites—and a few secular Sunnis as well—agree that the Mahdi Army at least balances the excesses, and the sometimes ultra-gruesome methods of the Sunni Arab resistance. Hussein sees the Mahdi Army as a question of sovereignty; "It's more like an idea. I am *Jaysh al-Mahdi*, He is *Jaysh al-Mahdi*. His brother is *Jaysh al-Mahdi...*" He emphasizes the social role of the Mahdi Army, "spontaneously helping people and trying to solve their practical problems."

Naturally Sadr City residents, in their natural habitat, do everything they can to downplay the other dark—and very real—side of the Mahdi Army: the sectarian killings, the "armed and dangerous mob on a rampage" element. On the other hand Sadr City will continue to live in constant fear of being attacked by more horrendous car and truck bombings. And there's of course "Amrika."

By the spring of 2007 the Pentagon had started spinning murky stories of "secret cells" in Sadr City loaded with EFPs (explosively formed penetrators), bombs made in Iran used in most attacks by the Mahdi Army against the US in Sadr City. Residents angrily denied it: they said the Americans are attacking the neighborhood, not the other way round; and they have nothing to do "with the Iranians." The Mahdi Army may have access to these bombs on the black market, but this does not mean they are being armed by Tehran.

The key problem is Shiite/Shiite violence. The Badr Brigades—these ones effectively trained by Iran's Revolutionary Guards—were now clashing with the Mahdi Army in Sadr City itself. This boiled down in essence to a rivalry between eminent families fighting for political hegemony—the al-Sadr and the al-Hakim. The fighting could expand—with horrific consequences. Muqtada issued orders for the Mahdi Army to cool down.

By the spring of 2007 the Sadrists were on the way to forming a popular front in a true revolutionary movement. They are pro-resistance; against federalism; and against too much de-Ba'athification (or "the return of the killers," as many a secular Shiite in Baghdad puts it). My impression was that Muqtada was building a parallel state right out of the ghetto. It was all boiling down to good old class struggle—between the bourgeois, al-Hakim-controlled SCII and the Sadrist popular masses. Muqtada was winning for obvious reasons: the bourgeoisie—collaborating with the occupation—was absolutely inept at government and Iraq was plunging into even more misery than sub-Saharan Africa. And no wonder this fierce Iraqi nationalist was such a bogeymen to American elites: the US imperial expansion had always been based on divide-and-conquer and the squashing of nationalist movements. Muqtada may be as much of a "thug" (as he is defined in the US) as Cromwell and Napoleon were in their time.

In Sadr City once again I had come face to face with the future of the Arab world: urban, young and poor, and Muqtada was their leader. It was easy to imagine Muqtada's followers reaching their maturity and finding no place at all in the new, post-everything world order—and getting very angry about it. It was easy to visualize the all-familiar fear   of Western elites when confronted to the beggars' banquet vociferously demanding better global wealth distribution—and not more Sharia law.

"Democracy"—or anything resembling it—would surge straight out of the Arab ghetto, or it would not surge at all.

As for "Amrika," I was once again convinced there's absolutely no way the US will conquer any hearts and minds amongst over half the population of Baghdad. And should the Pentagon, in desperation, go for the much-feared "battle of Sadr City," there would be only one way to yell "mission accomplished" all over again: by perpetrating a mass genocide.

13: The degree zero of culture

This was once the pinnacle of world culture. Al-Mustansariya Universi-ty is older than the Sorbonne. During Saddam, even with UN sanctions, it was still churning out the best and the brightest in Iraq. Sons of wealthy families in Lebanon, Jordan, the Emirates or northern Africa were still being sent by their parents to study in al-Mustansariya. Its reputation was sterling all over the Arab world.

Today young teachers at al-Mustansariya—who insisted on remaining anonymous, for their own protection—painted to me a bleak picture of university life. It all started way back in 2003. Most of the professors who had their PhD or Masters abroad went back to Western Europe or the US. The few ones that remained have just finished their higher education. "During Saddam they were all forced to enroll in the Ba'ath Party, that was the only way to get a job," says a teacher. "Almost all of them were in high positions." Immediately after the invasion and the beginning of the occupa-tion, many left to Syria and Yemen.

Then came the purges. The director of the Education Department was killed in 2003, as well as the heads of the Departments of Psychology and Literature. Sons of teachers were also killed—after their parents were fired. Almost all of the Law professors at the University of Baghdad were also killed. As for the University of Baghdad, in the Jadriya district, not related to al-Mustansariya, it is attended by a much higher percentage of Sunni Arab and Kurdish students.

Courses, anyway, remain on schedule. "But it's only theory, not prac-tice, there is no budget for it in Sciences," says a teacher. Classes run from 8:00 am to 11:30 am and then from 12:00 pm to 3:00 pm. At 4:00 pm every-thing is closed. Students still use the traditional white and gray uniform. In many cases students attend classes only once a week. "And the teachers never confront them," says a professor. After final examinations, everyone is approved. There are countless cases of students threatening teachers with a "bullet" message—a bullet wrapped in a piece of paper—in case they fail their exams. Copying and cheating during exams is commonplace. "The students can do anything they want," says a professor.

What many want basically is to finish their courses and leave Iraq as soon as possible. The refugee demand for Western European countries in neighboring Syria (especially for the new Holy Grail, Sweden) is gigantic, and chances are boosted with a higher education diploma.

Muqtada al-Sadr's Mahdi Army controls all the security arrangements at al-Mustansariya. Photos of Muqtada are naturally ubiquitous. There are a number of well educated Mahdi Army students—in Literature and Education. "But not many in the Faculty of Sciences," comments a teacher. The absolute majority of students nowadays come from Sadr City, Talbiya (an annex to Sadr city), New Baghdad and Palestine street—all Shiite areas. Not surprisingly, 90% of the students are Shiite, only 10% Sunni. A Psychology teacher says she is not allowed to discuss a lot of hot political and social issues. She is allowed though "to prevent disputes among students." There has been an express order by Muqtada al-Sadr that no Sunni professors should be executed—presumably by rogue Mahdi Army elements; in fact, they should be protected.

There is a bus station and a special entrance at the university for teachers, who carry a special ID, and a parking lot for the students. Everyone is searched at the entrance, but not thoroughly. Mobiles with cameras are OK—even though "all the bombings in this area are coordinated by mobile phone," says a teacher.

A simple monument at the entrance of the university celebrates the memory of the victims—mostly girls—of the horrific January 2007 bombing which killed 107 and wounded more than 280. Now female students attend classes twice a week maximum. The university still receives threats via the internet from Salafi-jihadists to "stop education." Snipers routinely shoot university guards. This is considered by Salafi-jihadists as a "Shiite university"—thus a prime target.

Whatever happens politically in Iraq, most of Sunni Baghdad—and even secular, educated Shiites—still fear Sadr City. It is undeniably a class struggle issue. This is manifest in the extremely derogative expression *chroqui* (loosely translatable as "bad person") applied to people from Sadr City. Or even worse: *meedi* (meaning "low class who used to live with cows"). Wealthy Baghdadis refer to most Shiites who come from southern Iraq—and settle in the teeming suburbs—as "dirty thieves." It would take a lot of Freudian and Jungian insight to analyse Sadr City's inferiority complex. Sunni taxi drivers, just like in Saddam's time, still refuse to take passengers to Sadr City ("it's full of kidnappers").

With final exams at al-Mustansariya over, there was the inevitable graduation ball—inside the university compound, of course. Most of the graduates were the "dirty thieves" of Sadr City. Democratization of culture or degree zero of culture? Call it the revenge of the excluded: the Mahdi Army will continue to be on a roll—sprinkled with university diplomas.

14: What Sistani wants

Popular wisdom in Iraq rules that Grand Ayatollah Sistani, with a simple *fatwa*, or even a single word, can bring the US occupation to an abrupt end. So why doesn't he? In the impossibility to pose this half-a-trillion-dollar question to the Grand Ayatollah himself (he does not grant interviews to foreigners, and never even bothered to receive US occupation authorities), the next best option is to talk to someone close to the *marjas* (sources of imitation) in Najaf.

To start with, there is ample controversy on how many *marjas* there are in Iraq, four or five. Four of them sit in Najaf, the Shiite "Vatican": Ali al-Sistani, al-Najafi, al-Mudarassi and al-Iaqubi. But there's also al-Khalse, who sits in Khadimiya, in Baghdad.

Sheikh Muhammad al-Roubaie is a top cleric at the Imam al-Rabani cleric organization, affiliated with the *marjaiyya*, which he defines as "the government of the people." He insists there is "no separation between religion and politics." He blames the current "crisis" on the fact that "people are not following the religious leaders. Religious thinking is responsible for solving people's problems. But not all learned men who put a turban are truly religious."

As in every conversation with a Shiite cleric, the conflict between the West and Islam is paramount, and every specific question is met with a cryptic, but sometimes enlightening, answer. Sheikh al-Roubaie insists that "when the West comes to Islam, those who do the work of God don't brandish a sword. We must explain to the world that Prophet Muhammad did not come to the world with a sword. Islam is a peaceful religion." Hence the objective of Sheikh al-Roubaie's organization—"to promote a better understanding of Islam." He says "we follow the prophet but also Jesus as a person, with his human qualities. We follow Islam in practice, not just by the word." The conversation is peppered with references to

Imam Ali's book, *Nahje al-Balaga* (there are very good English translations published in Iran).

Sheikh al-Roubaie says Sistani is like the principal in the *marjaiyya*. His rulings are obeyed "in general. But there are also the followers of individual *marjas*." Sheikh al-Roubaie startingly admits "there are differences among the *marjas*. Some think it's better for the Americans to stay, otherwise there will be civil war. Others think they should leave. There is no united opinion." Personally, he feels "bad" about the divergences.

According to the Sheikh, Sistani cannot issue a *fatwa* to get rid of the occupation because "he doesn't have such a privilege, he knows that a lot of people would die. The only one who would have such a privilege is Imam Mahdi." As Prophet Muhammad and the Imam Mahdi "are not situated in real life now and are thinking about more important things," it's unlikely Grand Ayatollah Sistani will ever directly tell Bush and Cheney to pack up and go.

Sheikh al-Roubaie believes the tens of thousands of Iraqis who are falling victim to the war and sectarian hatred are dying "for a reason"; "People have to be more spiritual. Still now there are people among us with Saddam in their minds. And the West thinks the West is perfect, has nothing to learn. People should recover their humanity without ethnic prejudice. And the killing will continue—even if the Americans go. There is no reason to believe there won't be any other ways of killing in the world."

Sheikh al-Roubaie believes Muqtada al-Sadr may also one day become a *marja*, "if the continues his studies in the *hawza*." Muqtada, of course, is still too young, his crucial "sin" even among Iraqis who sympathize with his positions. But the Sheikh observes that "now he is already as important as his father ever was." He let it escape that "only Sistani and al-Hakim" have a close relationship with the Maliki government—an observation that is a political treatise in itself. It means that what Sistani wants is the consolidation of SCII's political power.

61

Up to 2004, it was still possible to take a taxi in Baghdad, make a stop at Hilla and reach Najaf with no hassle. In another measure of the current "security" in Iraq, a trip to Najaf for a foreigner is now considered suicide. "Too dangerous." "You look *ajnabi* (foreigner). Worse still: "You look European." Or "You look Iranian, they [the Sunni guerrillas] will kill you."

As far as the security situation in the Shiite holy sites is concerned, SCII and its Badr Organization are in charge in Najaf and Karbala. The Mahdi Army is in charge in Kufa. Cleric Sayyed Mahmoud al-Saqhri also controls private guards in Karbala. There is no direct American involvement.

People recently coming from Najaf describe it as surrounded by checkpoints—all of them manned by Iraqi Army and police (overwhelmingly Shiites, mostly faithful to Badr). They stop and search all buses. All mobile phones must be left with the guards. All cars must be left at least 2 km away from Najaf's city centre, which houses Imam Ali's shrine. The only cars allowed are carrying coffins. The coffins themselves are uncovered and searched for bombs. "The guards are men, and they touch women's corpses," comments a horrified Najafi.

No one gets inside Imam Ali's shrine carrying coffins anymore—as it was customary. A side route must be taken leading to a side entrance to the sprawling Dahr-al-Islam cemetery. The souq adjacent to the shrine has been rebuilt—after continuous bombings. Commerce now "is normal." But the city is "too quiet, too silent." Kufa—the heart of Muqtada al-Sadr's movement—is regarded as "much busier."

Inside Imam Ali's shrine in Najaf there "are more Iranians than Iraqis"—all of them spies in the eyes of the Pentagon. These Iranian pilgrims simply cannot go to Kadhimiya in Baghdad or Samarra; the trip is far too dangerous. On the other hand suicide bombers—Salafi-jihadists—prefer to attack Karbala, because they are attacking the Mahdi Army directly.

Even with so much accumulated, overlapping grief, Sheikh al-Roubaie believes "a solution exists for the problems in Iraq—and for everything else.

It's simple. People should follow their true human qualities." One wonders if this would ever apply to people like Dick Cheney. Anyway the Sheikh remains optimistic for the future—even without a Sistani *fatwa*: "Religion is scientific. It's life. It's the cultivation of life."

15: The sanctions generation speaks

One of my fondest memories of a visit to Baghdad in the spring of 2002—when the axis of evil/WMD farce was already in full swing in the US—was spending long days on al-Mustansariya university talking to Sunni and Shiite students. They were all part of the sanctions generation—who grew up in the 1990s and early 2000s in deprivation and distress, courtesy of Washington and the United Nations. Even after so much suffering, they were never enraged. And even after being subjected to relentless demonization by the West but especially US armchair warriors, they would always finish our elaborate conversations suavely asking: "So, you still think we are an axis of evil?"

This time, thanks to Fatima, I was introduced to a new batch of the sanctions generation—older, wiser, and now in a post-Shock and Awe situation. They were still not enraged—at least on the surface. It's useful to remember with them what life was like in a country subjected to the most draconian sanctions of modern times. It's also useful to keep in mind that they will never, ever forget.

›℃

Mohammed Yassin Alian, 27, a college graduate on Economics and Administration, refused to go into exile. He still lives in Baghdad.

"During the nineties I was a teenager. My family consists of two sons and two sisters. My father was an employee in the state services, so was my mother. We were in good financial condition before the economic blockade imposed by the UN. But after that we began the torture journey of everyday life. Our money in the bank began to run out. My father's monthly salary was just 3500 Iraqi dinars and my mother's salary was 3000 dinars. It was never enough—because everything was expensive. For example, the cost of one kilo of meat was about 4000 dinars. Bread was too bad—no one could eat it... There was no sugar in the stores. The government had to prevent anyone from making and buying desserts."

"We lived only on the items in the ration card made by a committee of the UN. There was no milk or dairy products, or meat. We lived only on bread and rice. All our friends and neighbors suffered the same thing. The dollar became a very rare currency: one dollar was the equivalent of 3000 Iraqi dinars. Saddam's regime prevented everybody from dealing, buying or selling the American dollar. People started to migrate out of Iraq; many went to Jordan, which was the only country which had open borders with Iraq."

"Lots of families began to sell whatever they had at home—at the cheapest prices—so they would survive. My family was one of them. We even had to sell our most important things. I heard my mother complaining and my father answering 'What can we do?' Fuel was not expensive at that time—like it is now. So my father worked in his private car as a taxi driver and that has become a common situation in Iraq."

"At the start of each school year the state could not distribute new editions of books to schools; they had to be second-hand because all Iraqi factories were also affected by the blockade. Our parents couldn't buy school supplies to us so we were told to use old clothes. My mother adapted her clothes to suit my sister. People would start sending some of their sons outside of Iraq to find work, and they would send them some money. These people lived better than anybody else. Even the rich were in trouble—their factories had been halted for lack of raw materials because of the economic embargo. Property owners were affected because rents were cheap, but nevertheless they were better off than everybody else."

"We did not understand why our lives had become so dire; after all we used to live in much better conditions. At school we would only hear about the achievements of Saddam and the Ba'ath. Among friends we would only hear insults hurled at Saddam and sometimes at America, which was the reason behind all this hunger and poverty."

"Media was very limited at the time. There was al-Shabab TV station, run by Uday Hussein. Frankly the station was useful and had many diverse programs, new films, scientific reports. We would see the world through it, as cinemas and theaters had become so commercial, as my father said. The Iraqi films shown in cinemas and theaters were silly—all this because of the migration of large number of intellectuals at that time. That was also the case with professors and doctors who had graduated from European universities; they traveled to other countries for employment, particularly Yemen and Libya, which opened their doors to Iraqi university professors."

"I had a friend at school, his name was Ahmed, his father was I think from Tikrit, working with Saddam Hussein. His living conditions were completely different. He was always wearing new clothes and his pocket money was the equivalent of many large salaries. One day I visited him at home: everything was very modern and beautiful, and I was impressed with his computer. I asked my father to buy me one, the price was between US$ 600 to US$ 700, equivalent at that time to two million dinars, which meant great wealth. No one could own such a machine while not working in institutions that paid salaries in dollars or working with Saddam. My father's response was obviously a refusal. Things began almost to improve, but not too much, when oil for food was implemented. We began to feel a modest change through the purchase of new things and simple home stuff after we had been denied for so many years."

"There was a constant joke about Iraqis—that they are magicians. How can a family live for so many years on just one dollar per month—a strange thing. After that the situation has changed. But there is no safety now, we are no longer able to go to the parks in the city or go to see any games. We do not want money; we wish to live normally, as we lived even during those days of the embargo. We only want safety."

Hassan Ali Muhammad, 27, socially comes from the other side of the spectrum compared to Mohammed Alian.

"We are a poor family—consisting of my mother and father and my grandmother, three brothers and three sisters. We were all junior at the time. My father was a simple construction worker. Our condition was good before the embargo. But during it all work stopped and we really starved. So we sold out everything we had at home. My father tried to work as a bearer at Al-Shorgha market. Me and my brothers also tried to work to pay the rent of our home. My mother was forced to work in other people's homes. However this was not enough to live well."

"One of my friends asked me once to steal light things and sell them. But frankly I feared my father and did not agree with him. I knew that my friend, along with two slightly older friends, 12 to 13-years-old, were stealing whatever they found in the gardens of rich residential areas. They knew that if they were caught by the police they would be released, because they were too young."

"At the time police was corrupted; any person who killed or robbed could escape from prison by bribery. I recall an incident that a person was sentenced to death. His family exchanged him with a crazy person, paid to his family a large sum of money and bribed the police to have their son run away from prison; thus they executed the crazy person."

"Many gangs spread in our poor regions, but their activities were limited to stealing women's and men's handbags and also gold chains on women's necks. We all had to go to work in the morning and in the day on which there was no work there was no food. Saddam specifically was the reason, but America intended to make us starve. We were always hearing that there was a committee of the United Nations to help us, or ease the embargo on us, or they came for an inspection. But they were letting us down. I was seeing people who lived in affluent areas very well-off, how I wished to wear or eat just like them whenever I saw them in restaurants."

28-year-old Yunus Yassin was slightly better-off than Hassan Muhammad.

"I worked with my father, at that time, in an auto repair shop. I left school because it was not useful. I know friends who graduated from colleges, they had to work for free to survive. They were selling anything they had in the streets. Because of the blockade, which was preventing people from buying modern cars, we were reforming old cars and manufacturing new spare parts for different cars. We had to excel because the existing spare parts were not enough for everybody. Frankly we were better than others in terms of income; however, since the embargo was on all Iraq, we were also suffering as all the rest."

"The United States is the main reason of our suffering—they imposed sanctions on us. Saddam was part of the reason, no more, no less."

Yasmin Khodeir, 30, was an employee in a government department. She also has something to say about the awful health situation during the 1990s.

"Health conditions in general were awful, because food wasn't sufficient. A study showed that the physical structure for those who were born in 1991 and after was unhealthy. The structure of the bodies is small and weak; all this because of insufficient food. There was also the deficiency in medicines in pharmacies and hospitals; even if they existed, their quality was bad."

"People began to suffer, especially older people. Many sick people also died as a result of shortage of medicines. Even those who had chronic diseases that require continuous treatment suffered of this deficiency of medicines and died—especially those patients who had cancer by contamination that struck Iraq from American weapons."

"I remember a case in the hospital. An old man came to the hospital laboratory to make an analysis—too expensive at private laboratories, more than US$70. He was begging those who worked at the hospital to make the analysis because he couldn't afford to go to a private lab. But they couldn't help him, because all laboratory equipments were old. The man insisted, he was dangerously ill; so they took a sample from him despite their assurance that the result would be incorrect. Only very simple aid was provided by humanitarian organizations. America knew what was happening to us and did not do anything."

"At that time I was a little girl and like other girls I needed many things that my family was not able to provide. Some of my girl friends had relationships with rich people just to get money from them. Others married a man they didn't like, just because he had money, or because he was working with the foreign press agencies and taking a salary in dollars. Now, after the situation has changed, one of my friends regrets her marriage. Some families began marrying their daughters early—either for the money or to preserve their reputation."

"All these things were caused by the blockade and the lack of material and food resources, which led to deviant behavior. The main reason is the US, which wanted to kill the personality of the Iraqi citizen before murdering him physically."

"One of the results of the embargo was the creation of two classes. Most in the rich layer were Saddam's friends, or people close to him from the western region and Tikrit. They exploited young girls and women—and bought many of them. The second class was the poor people—most of them from the south; this was one of the methods of collective punishment after the uprising in the south."

"People complained not against Saddam alone, but also against the United States for its insistence on torturing and starving the Iraqi people. And this despite so many years having elapsed after the occupation of Kuwait."

16: Our true heart of darkness

There's a graffiti war going on in Baghdad. In Sunni neighborhoods the champions are "Saddam Hussein is a martyr" and "Muqtada is the leader of the thieves." In Shiite neighborhoods the favorite used to be "From Fallujah to Kufa Iraq won't be beaten down"; now "Fallujah" has been erased from the script. In Sadr City the favorite is "Down with the Ba'athists."

The Adhamiyah wall—the symbol of the Baghdad gulag, rejected by more than 70% of Iraqis—is not finished, but the neighborhood is already isolated by a cluster of checkpoints, with all major streets blocked by blast walls and barbed wire. Walls are planned to expand to Dora, Ghazaliyah, Amriya, al-Amel, al-Adl—a replication of Baghdad gulag practices in Fallujah, Tal Afar, Haditha, Samarra. The Amriya wall will be even *taller* than Adhamiyah's. Residents confirm Adhamiyah is also internally divided. The old area of al-Safina, nearby a cemetery, is now populated only by hardcore Sunni Arab families and Salafi-jihadists. The area known as Camp, between the Nida mosque and Officers street, is now infested with ferocious gangs bent on killing and kidnapping.

The local market has been virtually abandoned by civilians. Shops are open only two hours a day at most. House trading will continue to boom. Scouts search abandoned houses who they subsequently rent to guerrillas or displaced Sunni families. Some houses become prime weapons depots. The motorcycle rules as the only available means of transport. No taxi drivers dare to go to Adhamiyah. US soldiers will continue to raid houses no matter what.

But life somehow goes on. An educated Adhamiyah resident with a good sense of humor tells the story of how "the Americans are everyday on patrol. They search houses with their dogs. But one day one of their expensive dogs ran away"—along with his new, "local," non-pedigreed friends. In five minutes, a kid in the neighborhood self-described as "The Prince of Dogs" got the picture. "In 30 minutes he found the expensive

American dog." The dog liked him, and they are still together—to the despair of the Americans, who are still searching. Everybody apparently knows this story in Adhamiyah. They call the kid "Iraqi Ali-Baba." "But the kid will have to sell the dog in the market," adds the resident, because of the high maintenance. So this Gucci dog's destiny will turn out to be shabby souq al-Ghazil, already bombed several times.

The words of Sheikh al-Kobaisi, the assistant secretary-general of the powerful Sunni Arab Association of Muslim Scholars (AMS), to a crowd united to protest the Adhamiyah wall, will continue to resonate with most of Iraq's 5 million Sunnis. These were the Sheik's greatest hits: "Who has the power to bomb tanks will bomb this wall"; "Security does not come with tanks and missiles. It will come with the American departure"; "We have not attacked people who are inside the Green Zone. It's because of their deeds that we have become slaves."

An Iraqi government ad oozing Madison Avenue-style production values is shown incessantly on al-Iraqiya state TV, depicting a black-veiled suicide bomber about to blow up a street market. The punch line: "There is no religion in terrorism." It's not altering Salafi-jihadists' hearts and minds. No matter where the American surge leads Baghdad—the former prosperous capital of the eastern flank of the Arab nation—will continue to disintegrate into a cluster of decomposing urban tissues at war with each other.

The Mahdi Army will continue to balance the excesses of strands of the Sunni *muqawama* and the Salafi-jihadists, in an bloody operatic crescendo that would make Martin Scorsese green with envy. Even the Pentagon was forced to admit in the summer of 2007 that 52% of the people of Baghdad believe militias are defending their interests.

Karada is now virtually the only open market, with shops open during the day, in all of Baghdad—at least until the next bombing. For their part American convoys—moving at 5 km/h maximum with their "Danger" and "Stay back 100 meters" messages in large English and minuscule Arabic lettering—will continue to exasperate Baghdadi motorists and bring the city to a halt, not to mention being prime sitting ducks for IEDs, car bombers and snipers.

Attacks similar to the one on independent radio Digla will be replicated. The radio station is in Adjamiah—a Sunni neighborhood. A couple who managed the station, parents of a little girl, tell how the attackers, presumably Salafi-jihadists, threw a bomb in the garden. "No police showed up, although there are two checkpoints nearby." Then the attackers started shooting. The employees didn't leave the small two-storey building, and responded with their won Kalashnikov fire. The couple finally managed to escape. "But later the attackers stole a computer with information on all our employees. We're afraid they could be persecuted one by one."

In Heiten, another Sunni district, according to residents, the number of houses "inundated with weapons" and "perfect places to hide kidnapped people" is bound to increase. The *muqawama* in the area even told locals to evacuate a clinic because it could be bombed. In Amriya, any woman in the streets will not afford not to be wearing the *niqqab*, completely veiling her face. There will be more and more deadly clashes in Baya'a, in Karkh, on the eastern side of the Tigris, once an area that was a haven of Baghdad culture, now a Mad Max hell.

Snipers will continue to do brisk business. There was the Yemeni sniper of al-Shurta, in west Baghdad—who was on a steady killing diet of at least six people a day. When he was caught locals realized there was also a Sudanese sniper. And then came the sniper of al-Ra'y, who specializes in the al-Shabab area. There's even a "sniper school"—in al-Radwaniya. People in these affected neighborhoods cannot even dare to cross their own streets.

Al-Shurta itself was turned into a ghost town. But then the Mahdi Army moved in, occupying abandoned apartments, recruiting local youngsters and getting into gear to fight the al-Qaeda in Iraq jihadis based in feared nearby Radwaniya. Al-Qaeda in Iraq snipers made life in al-Shurta absolutely impossible. Local markets are totally deserted. The local Mahdi Army had to block any traffic to prevent a flurry of car bombings.

Al-Qaeda in Iraq—in its demented urban incarnations from Dora to Amriya and Radwaniya—will continue killing even fellow Sunni Arabs, especially harmless barbers (a grudge against un-Islamic haircuts) and garbage collectors (after all they are government employees). Uncollected piles of garbage—a recurrent theme in Baghdad—also offer the prospect of a perfect hideout for IEDs, mines and bombs.

The best time in Baghdad to circumvent the gigantic lines and have a tank filled with gas will continue to be immediately after a shooting spree—or a car/truck bombing. More and more mule carts—most carrying propane tanks—will be seen in the dusty streets among the rusty orange-and-white Passats and the sheep grazing by the curbside—heralding the return of Baghdad to the Middle Ages. The truce between the Iraqi Army and sections of the *muqawama* will also prevail: "Don't do anything against us"—say the guerrillas—"and we will not shoot you." The Army's poor souls anyway are more than ready to admit that they're only in it for the money—one of the few forms of steady salary available in the country.

Amid the daily deadly litany of car bombings, kidnappings, occupation reports in newspeak, votes in the US Congress, "special meetings," communiqués and al-Qaeda video specials, many people in Baghdad will still need to scrape US$80 a month for fuel, this when a teacher gets paid a maximum salary of US$200, and this in a country that holds 115 billion barrels of proven oil reserves. Half of the city will remain with no running water—millions of people sweating bricks under 53° C temperatures in high summer. Fathers and sons will be seen begging in tandem in the dusty streets to get a couple of dollars. The dream job will continue to be "taxi driver." The ultimate dream—exile in Sweden—will come with the exorbitant price of freedom: US$15,000. The running Baghdad joke already spells that in 2008 Sweden will become an Iraqi province.

Still, amid so much distress, we will still see the pages of Iraqi papers overflowing with poems—the mode of expression par excellence of Arab culture.

The federalists of SCIRI may have changed the party's name to SIIC and pledged their unconditional allegiance to revered Grand Ayatollah Sistani—but it's their Badr Brigades, including death squads, that will continue to lay down the law out of the 7th floor of the Interior Ministry. Meanwhile the nationalist Sadrists will continue to rule the Shiite street. As for how come Grand Ayatollah Sistani supports the new US-supervised Iraq oil law (SIIC does), which will virtually hand out Iraq's natural wealth to Anglo-American Big Oil, the Iraqi Parliament might as well listen to Iraq's unions—which threaten a "mutiny" if the law is approved. The unions describe the oil law as "a bomb that will kill everyone."

There will be countless more "mysterious" attacks on the Green Zone in the middle of the night. Residents nearby will hear loud explosions and see columns of smoke. A fleeting Reuters dispatch on the explosions will appear on the net, with no details, and then mysteriously vanish. Nearby residents are adamant: "The Green Zone is attacked with mortars every day." In May 2007 alone there were 39 (documented) attacks. And al-Qaeda in Iraq has not even taken its new al Quds 1 guided missile for a test drive.

The only thing Washington has to offer is a muddy Joint Campaign Plan developed by counterinsurgency ace Gen. David Petraeus, the top commandeer in Iraq, along with ambassador Ryan Crocker, to achieve "localized security" in Baghdad by June 2008 and a "broader sense of security" by June 2009. Darkness dawns at the break of noon: average Baghdadis say this is too little, too late. The UN says Somalia is now the most urgent humanitarian crisis on the planet. No it's not: it's Iraq. Baghdad is now the ultimate laboratory of perverse social engineering: a brutalized, militarized, neo-Spartan future three-tier society where privileges are enjoyed by the first tier—the US Army, the handsomely paid US shadow army of contractors—and the second tier—Iraqi politicians who spend most of their time in London or Middle Eastern capitals. The overall population are just corralled, humiliated and treated as mere slaves—extras in their own land.

According to Oxfam at least 8 million Iraqis are in a desperate situation—lacking, in the case of at least 1.2 million, even food to eat. 30% of children are malnourished. 92% suffer from learning problems. 70% in an overall population of 26.5 million have no adequate access to water (it was 50% after 12 years of UN sanctions, before the 2003 invasion). Only 20% have basic sanitation. The similarities with Gaza—a de facto Israeli gulag—are striking. But Gaza has been occupied for four decades. Iraq has been occupied for a little over four years.

Take Iraqi Airways, for instance. True, some of its pilots have been assassinated. The reservation system is manual. After getting to Baghdad International Airport (which locals still call "Saddam")—an obstacle course that involves endless checkpoints and body searches—we may wait for as long as half a day, or sometimes a full day, for a "scheduled" flight. "There is no schedule," comments a passenger. No flight departure panel either. And not a single shred of information. Meanwhile throngs of bulky contractors loaded with high tech gear are dutifully guided to their safe, scheduled, comfortable, on time flights to Saudi Arabia, Dubai or Kuwait. They are superior beings. They sport badges. The average population has no badge; they are infra-beings.

This is the picture of "normal life" for people like the helpless, affable Kurd who poses as Iraqi Foreign Minister, Hoshyar Zebari, as well as scores of high-minded US senators, Congressmen and vapid retired generals on CNN. Their pre-packaged, spun-to-the-word certainty is an astonishing insult to world public opinion's intelligence. Why they don't surge via Iraqi Airways on "Saddam" International, buy a cheap Korean portable generator and hit the Red Zone with no Kevlar vests, no bodyguards, no SUVs with tinted windows, no protecting Apaches circling overhead, to wallow in the joys of "normal life"?

Leaving Baghdad at night, past curfew time, in this sad spring of 2007, was one of the most devastating experiences of my life. There are just a few dim lights down on the ground—as if the former pride and splendor of Islam was enveloped in a shroud. The only moving object is—what else—a serpentine American convoy about to go on a search and destroy mission in "normal life." The Bush/Cheney half-a-trillion-dollar (so far) Iraq adventure razed to the ground an entire Arab state. Not just any Arab state; the cradle of civilization as we know it has been hurled back to medieval times (but with mobile phones for everyone; an Iraqna SIM card costs only US$ 10). The Bush administration Political Science Academy's neo-medievalism with a twist could be summed up thus: we invade Iraq and finish off Saddam's Ba'athist regime. Al-Qaeda in Iraq shows up. Then we align ourselves with the Ba'athists to smash al-Qaeda. Naw, too obvious. We align ourselves with Iran-trained militias to smash al-Qaeda. We lump any anti-occupation Sunni and any potential or real "insurgent" with al-Qaeda. And we photoshop Abu Ghraib: delegating torture to Iran-trained militias—after all they are already ensconced at the Ministry of Interior—will do wonders for our PR.

Blowback will be perennial: the sanctions generation—the angry young men who grew up deprived of everything (by the West) during the 1990s—will never, ever forget it. Even if the Iraqi Parliament eventually votes a timeline for the end of the occupation. It used to be Joseph Conrad's Congo: now Iraq is and will remain the true heart of darkness of the early 21st century. Forget about Russia or China; now, finally, Bush/Cheney, the military-industrial complex and assorted armchair warriors can finally be assured the US has found an enemy for life.

17: The second coming of Saladin

Damascus

> *The best lack all conviction*
>
> *While the worst are full of passionate intensity.*
>
> W. B. Yeats, *The Second Coming*

The discreet green-and-white tomb of the greatest warrior of Islam, Saladin—by the splendid Umayyad Mosque in the former seat of the caliphate—may be the ideal place to meditate on if, where and when Islam may be shaken again by the advent of a new Saladin, nine centuries after the illustrious deeds of the great Muslim general.

Saddam Hussein, not least because he was also from Tikrit (although Saladin was a Kurd), fashioned himself as the genuine article—fighting (twice) the infidel Christian armies of the US. He is now no more than a martyr for a minority. Osama bin Laden carefully fashioned his iconography as a cross between Saladin, Che Guevara and the Prophet Mohammed. But as in the immortal line in Francis Ford Coppola's *Apocalypse Now,* "his methods are unsound"; despite the marketing success in the expansion of the al-Qaeda brand, Osama will never be able to capture the collective conscious of the *ummah.*

The new Saladin might be the son of a Palestinian refugee victim of the *Nakhba* ("catastrophe") six decades ago. He might be a computer wizard too sophisticated to be tempted by al-Qaeda's Salafi-jihadism. He might be an angry young man straight out of the "sanctions generation" in Iraq—deprived of everything while he was growing up, courtesy of the "international community."

He won't be a tourism developer in Dubai, self-styled "city of captivating contrasts" (between the Western/Arab business elites and the South Asian slaves, maybe?) He won't be the pampered son of the Sunni business aristocracy in Damascus showing off his Porsche Cayenne. He won't be a billionaire international playboy posing as politician a la Saad Hariri in Beirut. He won't be a gas-dealing executive in gas nirvana Qatar.

Conditions are more than ripe for the advent of a new Saladin—after the *Nakhba*, the 1967 lightning Israeli victory against the Arabs, the failures of pan-Arabism, the occupation of Afghanistan and Iraq, the Israeli attack on Lebanon, the limited appeal of Salafi-jihadism, the non-stop stifling of nationalist movements by Western-backed brutal dictatorships/client monarchies.

When the future Saladin looks at the troubled and dejected Middle East, the first thing he sees is Dick Cheney shopping for yet another war—skipping the "axis of evil" (Iran, unofficial member Syria) and ordering support from the "axis of fear" (Saudi Arabia, Egypt, Jordan, Kuwait, the Emirates) in his relentless demonizing of Iran. After inflating sectarianism in Iraq, this time the imperial "divide and rule" weapon of choice is Arabs vs. Persians.

The Bush administration may have taken a leaf from former colonial power France—which invented Greater Lebanon as a confessional state, thus prone to perennial turbulence—to apply it in Iraq. But plunging Iraq into civil war to control it better is not enough (and there's still the matter of securing the oilfields).

Forcing a practically de facto partition of Iraq into three warring crypto-states—a Kurdistan, a southern "Shiiteistan" and a small central, oil-deprived Sunnistan—mired in a sea of blood in the heart of the Middle East is not enough. For Cheney, the industrial-military complex and assorted Ziocon (Zionist/neo-conservative) warriors, the big prize is the subjugation of Iran. Because Iran, apart from its natural wealth, is the only power capable—at least potentially—of challenging regional US hegemony.

Yet the trademark Cheney threats—with the standard high-tech aircraft-carrier background—are not cutting much ice. Al-Jazeera has been rhetorically bombarded by everybody and his neighbor—from retired

Egyptian generals to Emirati political analysts—stressing that the Middle East will not support another US war. Iranian President Mahmoud Ahmadinejad, in a swift move, went to the United Arab Emirates—the first visit by any Iranian leader since the Emirates became independent in 1971, and all the more crucial because of a still-running dispute over a bunch of Persian Gulf islands.

The House of Saud—for which the only thing that matters is its own survival—desperately wants a solution as soon as possible for the Palestinian tragedy, before they may be buried six feet under by the terrible sandstorms blowing from Mesopotamia (think of hordes of battle-hardened Salafi-jihadis coming home after fighting the US in Iraq).

King Abdullah is not bent on antagonizing Iran. On the contrary: the most important guest at the much-ballyhooed Riyadh conference was Iranian Foreign Minister Manoucher Mottaki. Saudis and Iranians want to prevent US-provoked sectarianism in Iraq from spreading regionally. And King Abdullah wants a better deal for Sunni Arab Iraqis (hence his identification of Iraqi Prime Minister Nouri al-Maliki as an Iranian puppet).

While Cheney wants to pit Saudi Arabia against Iran, a discreet, behind-the-scenes Saudi-Iranian pact of no aggression may be all but inevitable. Saudi Foreign Minister Prince Saud al-Faisal said as much on the record: "Stop any attempt aimed at spreading sectarian strife in the region."

Iran of course can be very persuasive, holding some tasty cards up its sleeve—such as hard-earned intelligence directly implicating the Saudis in training the Sunni Arab *muqawama* (resistance) in Iraq on explosive form penetrators (EFPs), which the Pentagon foolishly insists come from Iran. Everyone in Iraq knows it is operatives from "axis of fear" allies Saudi Arabia and Egypt—and also Pakistan—who have provided the Sunni Arab guerrillas in Iraq with technology and training on improvised explosive devices and EFPs.

Thus we have another Bush administration foreign-policy special: Cheney coddling guerrilla-arming Sunni Arabs—who are facilitating the killing of American soldiers in Iraq—to support an attack on Shiite Persians (allied with the Iraqi Shiites supported by the Americans ...)

Anyway, Iraqi Shiites are more than winning the US surge game. The surging US soldiers are fighting various strands of the Sunni Arab resistance and al-Qaeda in Iraq. Meanwhile, the officially ensconced Badr Organization and its shady death-squad spinoffs are free to apply a lot of deadly pressure on the Sunni Arab civilian population. The Mahdi Army, on Muqtada al-Sadr's orders, just lies low—not taking the bait of fighting the Americans. Nothing will change the reality of this surge picture in the next few months.

A possible Saudi-Iranian entente would be a classic case of local powers taking the destiny of the region in their own hands. In a parallel register, in southern Beirut—prime Hezbollah territory—there are plenty of banners in front of buildings destroyed by Israel in the summer of 2006. They read: "The Zionist enemy destroys, the Islamic Republic of Iran builds."

Unity in the Muslim world is not a chimera: crypto-scientific Western babble of the "Arabs are extinct" variety is plain silly, as are nonagenarian Bernard Lewis's pontifications on the "clash of civilizations"—the "perhaps irrational but surely historic reaction of an ancient rival against our Judeo-Christian heritage." The new Saladin would tell Lewis to get a grip on reality and admit that the unabated political repression, tremendous social inequality and prevailing economic disaster all over the Middle East are direct consequences of decades of "divide and rule" Western imperialism plus some extra decades of non-stop meddling coupled with rapacious, arrogant and ignorant local elites.

The new Saladin knows how the US and Britain initially supported the Muslim Brotherhood—and then the Brotherhood supported the birth of Hamas. He knows how the US and Britain initially supported Iranian clerics—especially the late Ayatollah Khomeini—against the Shah. He knows how the US and Britain initially supported the Taliban. The aim was always to stifle any form of progressive, secular movement by socialists, communists or Arab nationalists.

A possible Saudi-Iran entente is still a dream. There is the parallel emergence of a coalition of top members of the "axis of fear"—Saudi Arabia, Egypt, Jordan—with Turkey and, of all players, Israel. Common objective: the containment of Iran. And not only Iran, but also Hezbollah and Hamas. King Abdullah was persuaded of this strategy by notorious Prince Bandar bin Sultan, aka "Bandar Bush," former Saudi ambassador in the US for 22 years, a close friend of both Bush and Cheney, and now the head of the Saudi National Security Council.

The strategy was in fact masterminded by a pedestrian version of the Four Horsemen of the Apocalypse: Cheney; Bandar; US deputy national security adviser Elliott Abrams; and former US ambassador in Iraq and Afghan jack-of-all-trades Zalmay Khalilzad. What the popular masses in the Middle East think about this is of course irrelevant. In majority-Sunni Egypt, for instance, the most popular politicians are by far Hezbollah's Sheikh Nasrallah, Khalid Meshal from Hamas, and Ahmadinejad. Two Shiites and a Sunni amply supported by Shiites.

Now about that "war on terror." The Bush administration is cunningly trying to spin the theme of "Sunni solidarity" to push the dagger of *fitna* (dissent) even further into the heart of Islam, always focusing on the same target: total, unchallenged domination of the Middle East.

Cheney could not but have also enlisted Pakistani President General Pervez Musharraf (who facilitates US intelligence on countless covert ops inside southeastern Iran organized from Balochistan in Pakistan). Some players are getting itchy, though. Turkey had to announce on the record that it would not join any "anti-Shiite alliance." Turkey cannot afford to antagonize Iran—not with the referendum on the autonomy of Iraqi Kurdistan.

The new Saladin also sees that the "war on terror" is far from over—metastasized into more subtle forms of Islamophobia, and still directly related to the attempted oil grab in the "big prizes" of Iraq and Iran. The privileged strategy to conquer fabulous natural wealth in the lands of Islam has been predictable from the start; building a case against the "barbarian," "uncivilized" and "pre-modern" Muslim world; vilifying Islam as a religion and Muslim culture and mores; promoting de facto discrimination and in may cases outright racism against Muslims in the wealthy North; equating Islam with terrorism.

The new Saladin knows it as much as virtually the whole 1.5-billion-strong *ummah* knows it.

And then there's the Shiite world. As long as US so-called elites fail to understand the phenomenal power of Shiism, any brilliant armchair strategy they cook up is destined to fail miserably.

Shiites in Iraq will never be co-opted by any US agenda—no matter the Himalayas of wishful thinking involved. They will never sacrifice their collective consciousness—forged by oppression and exclusion—nor their profound sense of historic victimization to the benefit of a made-in-America "liberal" utopia. Shiites will continue to stress their tremendous hostility to Zionism; to their society being corrupted by Western—especially US—popular and trash culture; and most of all to imperial designs on Muslim lands and natural wealth. It's in the DNA of Shiites to see themselves as the guardians of true Islam.

෨

So where will the new Saladin come from?

He could be Sheikh Nasrallah—who forced the formerly mighty Israeli army to back off, and who will inevitably prevail in a majority government in Lebanon through democratic elections.

He could be a young Sadrist who has never entered the Green Zone, and who before that was a member of the "sanctions generation," growing up in absolute marginalization. Now he goes to al-Mustansiriya University in Baghdad, he will get his diploma, and he will be better equipped to fight for the true liberation of Iraq. He could be Muqtada al-Sadr himself—the legitimate popular leader of a national-liberation movement.

He could be the son of a Palestinian refugee who grew up in Damascus or Beirut, got an education, emigrated to Canada to perfect his skills, learn from the best the West has to offer, and then one day come back and enter politics with a vengeance.

He could be a Muslim Brotherhood intellectual in Syria. He would fully back the Sunni Arab resistance in Iraq. He would fully back deposing the Hashemite monarchy in Jordan. He would fully back Hamas. As a Muslim Brotherhood Saladin, he would fight for a Sunni Arab Greater Syria capable of talking some sense into Israel.

He could be a Saudi-trained Sunni Arab sniper in Baghdad who posts his killing videos as manifestos on the Internet.

Or he could even not be an Arab, but a Persian—a resistance hero in case of a tactical nuclear US strike.

The soul of Saladin may be impatient for an heir. So are hundreds of millions in the *ummah*. What rough warrior, its hour come out at last, slouches toward Jerusalem, Damascus or Baghdad to be born?

Coda: On levitating the Pentagon

Paris

> *I read the news today oh boy.*
>
> *The Beatles, A Day in the Life, 1967.*

> *The only enemy of Iraq is the occupation.*
>
> *Muqtada al-Sadr, 2007.*

I left Baghdad (with a break in Damascus) and landed in Paris (with a break in Bangkok), smack into the Summer of Love remixed. Or was it? Forty years ago down in sunny Monterey, California, an ultra-cool black cat from Seattle named James Marshall Hendrix had set the world on fire. *Respect* by Aretha Franklin (written by Otis Redding) was the No. 1 hit single in the US (to be replaced, a month later, by *Light My Fire* by The Doors). Hendrix and Otis in Monterey merged into the Summer of Love—the apotheosis of Make Love Not War, vinyl treasures and Indian mottoes dressed in caftans and granny dresses, Israel's lightning victory in the Six-Day War merging into the escalation of the Vietnam War.

Today we had the sublime Patti Smith singing covers of Hendrix, Jefferson Airplane and the Beatles, Iraq burning instead of Vietnam burning and US/ Israeli Ziocons—led by Dick "Darth Vader" Cheney—mulling an attack on Iran. Call it the Summer of Hate.

Pentagon nemesis Muqtada al-Sadr, wearing a white shroud over his black cloak (meaning he was not afraid of dying), was spectacularly back from occultation, live from Kufa, straight out of his carefully protected Najaf (not Iran) seclusion. His nationalist, Islamic, non-sectarian message embodied the Iraqi street sandstorm that renders the occupation blind: "I renew my demand for the occupiers to leave or draw up a timetable for withdrawal, and I ask the government not to let the occupiers extend the occupation even for one day."

෪

Forty years ago, already in the spring of 1967 a stirring wave of counter-culture fusion between London and San Francisco was proving to be irresistible. Dismissed Harvard sage Tim Leary ordered everyone to "turn on, tune in, drop out" (The Beatles, already in 1966, were quoting from Leary's version of *The Tibetan Book of the Dead*—"turn off your minds, relax and float downstream").

While the radically politicized were yelling "Kill the pigs!" the Beatles were inventing whole new groovy sounds in the studio and enlightened beat poet Allen Ginsberg was singing the praise of Bob Dylan's victims in *Chimes of Freedom*—while assisting LSD experiments unsupervised by the CIA.

The irretrievably fragmented consciousness of the whole Western world was unifying, at least in the hearts and minds of young people everywhere, even for a fleeting moment in time. It was a river flowing out of the postwar consumer boom, from jazz to the beats to rebels without a cause to Dylan to The Beatles.

The Grateful Dead loved Ginsberg's *Howl* (from 1955) so much they set it to music. The doors of perception were being cleansed by what Ginsberg defined as "the divine herbs and greases" and by LSD—the crucial catalyst.

Yippie icon Abbie Hoffman, who defined The Beatles' *Sgt Pepper's* as "Beethoven coming to the supermarket," later recalled that "at the height of the American Empire we had all the bombs, all the cops in the world—and it was all ours—the Cadillacs, the two-car garages, the split-level ranch houses."

But then young people, spiritually unfulfilled, started to think there might be something else. Flower power met the East, met unbounded optimism—before, in 1968, reality came crashing down and despair set in.

85

Today Leary's motto would be "turn off, tune out, drop dead." At the decline of American Empire, young people have all the bombs, all the post-9/11 cops in the world—and it is not theirs. They have Hummers, holidays in Cambodia, neo-Byzantine condos. But then, spiritually unfulfilled even though they have been to all the five-star healing spas in the world, they still think there is nothing else—apart from a shot at TV celebrity.

Nobody gives a damn: the best lack all conviction (and take refugee in their iPods) while the worst simply lord over all, unchallenged. In overwhelmingly dumbed-down global medialand, an airhead heiress is the Queen of News, governments are no more than "political commissars of economic power," in the formulation of Portuguese Nobel Prize winner Jose Saramago, and the Bush administration and the industrial-military complex merrily fight proxy wars in Islamic lands.

History does repeat itself—as farce. By early 1967, the US had half a million troops in Vietnam. Massacres of civilians and torture—the precursors of Abu Ghraib—were routine. Half a million Vietnamese—the precursors of Iraqis—had already been killed. President Lyndon Johnson, another regular guy from Texas, was not going to "negotiate with terrorists."

Vietnam was being destroyed with napalm and Agent Orange. Laos had been bombed for three years without the US Congress even knowing about it (during the Nixon administration the victim would be Cambodia). By the Summer of Love, young people everywhere in the affluent West—and all around universities in the satellite global South—already knew the Vietnam War was no less than undiluted state-sponsored terror.

Muhammad Ali refused the draft—joining the throngs of "hell, no, we won't go." No one could possibly come up with a sound reason for shooting unknown Asians in far-off jungles (as if there is a good reason for shooting unknown Arabs in far-off deserts). The Vietcong were regarded as true freedom fighters (as were the Afghan mujahideen by Ronald Reagan in the mid-1980s, as are Sunni or Shiite Iraqi nationalists today).

Hippies and blacks were uniting against the Man (the white, conservative system)—but unfortunately there was not a lot of communal action, as blacks increasingly started feeling themselves members of a separate nation led by Eldridge Cleaver, Huey Newton, Bobby Seale and Stokely Carmichael. The year 1967 in San Francisco, London and Amsterdam was not exactly multi-racial: it was in essence a white phenomenon.

But politics did cross culture. Jean-Paul Sartre and Bertrand Russell became the executive and honorary presidents of a war-crimes tribunal set up in Sweden to try the US government for its crimes in Vietnam, including dropping more bombs than in the entire World War II, unleashing chemical poisoning and herding more than 8 million peasants into barbed-wire gulags. The tribunal had two sessions—in May and then in November 1967. In his speech, read by his American secretary, Bertrand Russell, in pure beat/countercultural mode, said:

> We have no armies and no gallows. We lack power, even
> the power of mass communication. It is overdue that those
> without power sit in judgement over those who have it ...
> We are responsible before history.

Never in Western civilization had a war been stopped by public pressure—in fact, the pressure of a whole generation—like the Vietnam War. Then there was a book—*The City in History* by Lewis Mumford, in which the Pentagon is described as an ancient malignant structure that has to be destroyed to ensure a peaceful world. Magic realism met political theater. Why not try to exorcise and levitate the Pentagon?

Abbie Hoffman dropped in to visit the malignant structure, measured it, got arrested—but also got a lot of free publicity. The happening took place on October 21, 1967. Norman Mailer, who immortalized 1967 in *Armies of the Night*, reflected on how totalitarianism breeds apathy: there was no confrontation at the gates of the Pentagon because the Man had channeled the protesters—a mix of new yippies and ex-hippies, dressed from native American to all shades Eastern—toward an empty parking lot. But the ceremony proceeded. Ed Sanders of The Fugs chanted a magical sort of mantra—to the sound of bells, cymbals, drums and brass.

> *In the name of the generative power of Priapus, in the name of totality, we call upon the demons of the Pentagon to rid themselves of the cancerous rumors of the war generals, all the secretaries and soldiers who don't know what they're doing, all the intrigue, bureaucracy and hatred, all the spewing coupled with a prostate cancer in the deathbed. Every Pentagon general lying alone at night with a tortured psyche and an image of death in his brain, every general lying alone, every general lying alone. Out Demons, out, Out Demons, out.*

The times they-are-a-changin' ... not. Where are the Bertrand Russell-style tribunals now? Where are the civic consciousness and the responsibility toward history of bloated pop stars, financial-system moguls and celebrities hawking their own line of clothing? Now more than ever, a triumph of the imagination is needed. The only way to stop the insanity of the Iraq—and soon Iran—war is through total, visceral mobilization of US public opinion.

Only mega-successful levitation would force the Pentagon to get rid of its must-list of four "enduring bases" (whatever the costs) in Iraq: al-Asad Air Base in Anbar province; sprawling Balad Air Base, with attached Camp Anaconda in the Sunni belt; Tallil Air Base in the south; and Camp Qayyaragh near Irbil, Kurdistan. And we're not even talking of the three Baghdad bases—Camp Victory (adjacent to Baghdad, formerly Saddam Hussein International Airport); Camp Taji (25 km north); and of course the 10-square-km, hit-every-day-by-mortars Green Zone, which is a base in itself containing the Vatican-sized, 40-hectare, biggest embassy in the world.

Both the White House and the Pentagon have confirmed on the record what every distressed observer of the Iraq tragedy already knew: this is naked Empire on steroids, aiming at securing control over Iraq's oil wealth and establishing permanent bases to control the Pentagon-denominated "arc of instability" from the Middle East to Central Asia.

As the Summer of Hate got into full swing Pentagon supremo Robert Gates stressed the "Korea model" and the US bent on securing a "long and enduring presence" in Iraq. And then White House spokesman Tony Snow reconfirmed that this is what President Bush wants and needs to fight "the larger war on terror."

Blowback is a given: more and more Shiites will actively support the Sunni Arab, Iraqi nationalist guerrillas, and they may be supported in their cause by Iranian Shiites as well. Pentagon desperation—or cunning—is evident in the fact there are no more holds barred now to divide Sunni and Shiite to project an appearance of ruling.

The Bush administration and its neo-con advisers' latest not-so-covert plan was to convince US public opinion of a nebulous Iranian government-Iraqi guerrilla connection—in plain English, another pre-packaged lie (echoes of Vietnam, echoes of Iraq). This carefully manufactured lie would establish the precious *casus belli* to bomb Iran. Call it Bombing Iran as an Extension of Destroying Iraq.

Forty years after the levitation of the Pentagon, there's no "democracy" to speak of anywhere. This is a plutocratic world. There's no formidable push to change the world for the better anywhere—but there are already rumblings of repressed anger from all corners of the global South, capable of exploding like a thousand volcanoes.

Virtually every Iraqi I spoke to in Baghdad—Sunni or Shiite—had no time for "your democracy," imposed or not by F-16s, demystifying it for what it is: a carefully fabricated illusion where the ultra-wealthy haves concentrate all the powers to inform, distract, vigil, cure, teach, decide and accumulate. Slovenian philosopher Slavoj Zizek evaluates how hard it is today to think of a credible alternative to the current system: "Thanks to all these Hollywood movies and the catastrophic scenarios depicted by ecologists, it is easier today to imagine a total catastrophe destroying all life on Earth than a radical change in social life. In sum, an asteroid touches the Earth, but capitalism survives."

In 1967, the Pentagon did not engage in liftoff. It did not turn pink. But the 1967 levitation ceremony at least gave the world the indelible poetic metaphor of a rose down the barrel of a M16—and the flowers dropping from the helmets of trembling 21-year-old soldiers. The Pentagon was humbled, anyway. It was—at least metaphorically—levitated. And the US—losing any intellectual support from its elites—started losing the war on Southeast Asians for good. It was a triumph of the human imagination over heavy-metal greed.

The whole world is baffled at how more than 60%—and counting—of US public opinion is against the Iraq war while at the same time there's no rage exploding in the American street. Could US public opinion—or at least the iPod generation—muster the will, the commitment and the courage to create a truly national anti-war movement and "levitate" the Pentagon all over again?

As we wait, our Summers of Love are now Summers of Hate. It fits; after all, when faced by the Masters of War, as the sublime Patti Smith sings it, we are all rock'n roll niggers. Niggers indeed: as the wealthy North was distracted by the ritual, annual fun-in-the-sun holiday season, the Bush administration hush-hushed a US$60 billion "military aid package" to Saudi Arabia, Egypt and Israel, US$ 13 billion of which to the very-much-in-need Saudi royal family. The package amounts to US$250 contributed by every American, or US$10 by every human being alive.

The official reason for the bonanza, according to Bush administration pet Afghan and current US ambassador to the UN Zalmay Khalilzad, is that "Saudi Arabia and others are not doing all they can to help us in Iraq." If Saudi royals can do nothing and have all the fun, why not the rest of us? So instead of levitating the Pentagon, every citizen of the planet, to the sound of *All You Need is Love,* should rather stand up and fight for his or her right of possessing an Apache, a Bradley, a machine-gun-mounted Hummer or—so sexy!—a born-to-be-wild exploding cruise missile. See ya on the next surge.

An Excerpt from *Globalistan: How the Globalized World Is Dissolving Into Liquid War*

By Pepe Escobar (Nimble Books, 2007)

To purchase Globalistan, *go to your favorite online bookseller or ask your local bookstore to order a copy via Ingram. The ISBN is 0978813820.*

1: IT DON'T MEAN A THING IF IT AIN'T GOT THAT EURASIAN SWING

History is a nightmare from which I am trying to awaken.

—James Joyce, *Ulysses*

... I saw the Aleph, from all points I saw in the Aleph the earth and in the earth once again the Aleph and in the Aleph the earth, I saw my face and my viscera, I saw your face, and I felt vertigo and I cried, because my eyes had seen this secret and conjectural object, whose name men usurp but which no man has seen: the inconceivable universe.

—Jorge Luis Borges, *The Aleph*

GENERAL JACK D. RIPPER: Mandrake, do you recall what Clemenceau once said about war?

GROUP CAPT. LIONEL MANDRAKE: No, I don't think I do, sir, no.

GENERAL JACK D. RIPPER: He said war was too important to be left to the generals. When he said that, 50 years ago, he might have been right. But today, war is too important to be left to politicians. They have neither the time, the training, nor the inclination for strategic thought. I can no longer sit back and allow Communist infiltration, Communist indoctrination, Communist subversion and the international Communist conspiracy to sap and impurify all of our precious bodily fluids.

—**Stanley Kubrick's** *Dr. Strangelove*

In his short story The Aleph Jorge Luis Borges—that South American Buddha in a grey suit—leads his narrator to discover "the place where we find, without confusion, all the places in the orb, seen from all of the angles" in the basement of a house in Buenos Aires. For the past few years I have had a feeling that the Aleph might be found in Iran, perhaps in fabled Isfahan, the pearl of Shah Abbas which in the 17th Century reached its full splendor, impressed in the famous rhyme Esfahan nesf-e jahan ("Isfahan is half the world").

Perhaps the Aleph would be in the Meidun, the fabulous square built in 1612—the Persian answer to Saint Mark's in Venice. Perhaps inside Sheikh Lotfollah mosque, whose intricately-painted dome tiles progressively change color from cream to strong pink as the days wear out and the light reflection forming the tail of a legendary painted peacock on the dome's roof also, imperceptibly, moves. We may spend hours, days, light-years absorbing this living meditation on the architecture of light. The peacock's tail inside an Isfahani mosque, now that would be a smashing location for the Aleph.

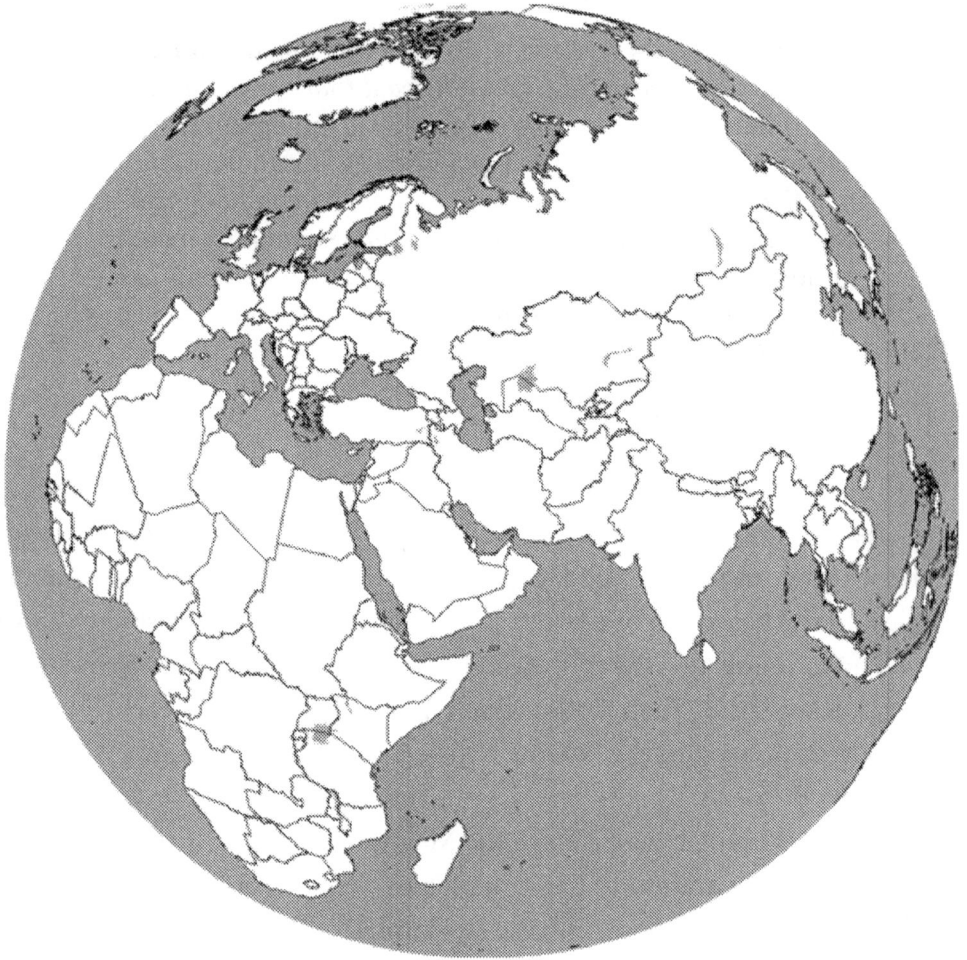

Figure 1. The world centered on Isfahan.

And why not? After all, Isfahan is at the center of Eurasia, roughly equidistant from Paris and Shanghai. And Eurasia is the geopolitical pivot of the world. Would the Aleph be there, it would be nothing but echoing the great 12th Century Persian poet Nezami Ghandjavi, who in the famous

Haft Peykar ("The Seven Portraits") wrote that "The world is the body and Iran is its heart."

Iran is at the key intersection of the Arab, Turk, Indian and Russian worlds. It's at the key intersection of the Middle East, Central Asia, the Caucasus, the Indian subcontinent and the Persian Gulf. It sits between three seas—the Caspian, the Persian Gulf and the sea of Oman. It's not far from Europe (in fact it will border Europe if and when Turkey accedes to the E.U.). And it's a neighbor to Asia (in fact it is in Southwest Asia). Iran is the ultimate crossroads in the heart of Eurasia.

Now about that oil, gas, Persian Gulf, Arabian Sea and Caspian Sea node. Not for nothing *Khalij-e-Fars*, in Farsi, means exactly "Persian Gulf." So Iran—the largest, most populous and most stable nation of Southwest Asia, strategically straddling most of the world's oil and gas reserves—is at the ideal crossroads for the distribution of oil and gas to South Asia, Europe and East Asia as both China and India emerge as two of the 21st Century superpowers. That is, Iran is the Great Prize *par excellence*. Maybe a larger than life Aleph.

Now suppose you are the world's only superpower with a foreign policy hijacked by neocons of the armchair warrior kind. What you're gonna do? You're gonna declare that you want regime change in Iran—betraying your dream scenario of relieving a puppet in power just like that former tortured soul, the Shah Reza Pahlavi.

Iran is completely surrounded by U.S. military bases in the Gulf, in Pakistan, in Afghanistan, in Turkey, in Central Asia, in Iraq, in Cyprus, and in Turkey, not to mention Israel, a naval base in Oman close to the hyperstrategic Strait of Hormuz (transit point of half the oil sold globally) and another, naval and air base, in the Indian Ocean, in Diego Garcia. Not that Iranian public opinion is particularly freaking out. Osama bin Laden, riding his Flying Carpet One cross legged with a giant F-16 breathing on his neck, side by side with a map of Iran surrounded by Uncle Sam's big guns: that was the cover of a magazine on political studies I found at the University of Tehran only a few months after George W. Bush's first Axis of Evil speech.

U.S. Global Strike planning is able in half a day to smash over 10,000 targets simultaneously in Iran in just one mission using "smart" conventional weapons carried by more than 200 strategic bombers (B-52s, B-1s, B-2s and F-117As). This would mean an even deadlier remix of Shock and Awe over Iraq—destroying the bulk of the political, military, economic and transport infrastructure of Iran. Some "minor" complementary issues should be added on, like mini-nukes redefined as "defensive weapons" thus "safe for civilians" because "the explosion is underground," as well as what Israel would be doing with some 5,000 "smart air launched weapons" it bought from the U.S., including 500 BLU 109 bunker busters.

Who actually wants this mini-Armageddon unleashed over the descendants of Cyrus the Great and Darius I? We find a sort of coalition (of the willing) special interests camouflaged behind national interests, linking Pentagon civilians of the armchair warrior kind, neocons in key government positions, an array of pro-Israeli organizations, Armageddon believers (call them Western Taliban), a great deal of the U.S. mainstream media and a minority of U.S. citizens. Neocons dismiss the International Atomic Energy Agency (IAEA), which is adamant: Iran's civilian nuclear energy program has no military wing. Neocons dismiss the CIA, which has made clear that any possible Iranian WMD would not materialize before 2015. Neocons have even cynically abandoned their "freedom agenda" for the Middle East. No more democracy-inducing Shock and Awe: what's left is just pure Jack D. Ripper logic.

Against mini-Armageddon on Iran we find a majority of retired U.S. military officials, Big Oil (for which, on a cost/benefit basis, this is very bad business), virtually all the Christian and Muslim organizations, the majority of U.S. public opinion and virtually all of the world's public opinion.

These special interests bent on mini-Armageddon derive outstanding business profits from one of the key intersections of Globalistan: globalization and war. In the Middle East the economic interests of the U.S. military-industrial complex happen to merge with the geopolitical interests of *Eretz Israel* (Greater Israel) proponents. During the binary, bipolar Cold War the U.S. rationale was to fight the communist specter. In Globalistan the specter remixed are the barbaric hordes of "Islamo-fascist" terror, Axis of Evil states, "rogue" states and failed states (after all "rogue" states are easier to locate on a map than "terrorists"). As informed Americans are well aware institutional framework and respectability for this agenda is provided by a plethora of militaristic, jingoistic think tanks which work closely with the Pentagon, the industrial-military complex and the powerful Israeli lobby (which could be described as a junior partner in this association).

The neocons profited immensely from 9/11 and the subsequent, nonsensical "war on terror" (which basically—literally?—means war on war). But the mighty profiteer of the neocon drive was actually the U.S. Corporatistan node of the military-industrial complex. Moreover the U.S. ruling class gets paid in tax money by the lower classes; that could not have been a more cunning mechanism of wealth distribution (1% of Americans control 40% of the country's wealth). Of all key neocon players a majority are former executives, consultants or shareholders of major Defense contractors. Think tanks may predominate in the (non) debate of ideas. But those really calling the shots are the military-industrial complex. This is all about business—not ideology. And Long, infinite, permanent war is an extremely profitable business.

The mini-Armageddon over Iran would mean the fulfillment of most dreams outlined in *Rebuilding America's Defenses*, the supremacist roadmap concocted by the warmongering neocon think tank Project for a New American Century (PNAC) in 2000, which could be defined as the Cheney/Wolfowitz roadmap. The "direct imposition of U.S. 'forward bases' throughout Central Asia and the Middle East" has been accomplished— sort of. But preventing the emergence of any potential "rival" or any viable alternative to "free market economy" implies smashing Iran. Further on down the militaristic road there's the "revolution in military affairs" (RMA), which is obsessed with the accumulation of high tech weapons systems for pulverizing infrastructure, but not interested in conquering hearts and minds; the "Strategic Defense Initiative"; and the total militarization of space. "Preemptive war" has already been further enhanced in the March 2005 Pentagon National Defense Strategy, to the benefit of "proactive war." Amid all this frenzy the Council on Foreign Relations was forced to admit, at its 2005 annual conference, that by 2010 the U.S. "will be spending more money than the rest of the world on defense."

By the summer of 2006 all the—ominous—signs were "on the table" (copyright Donald Rumsfeld) for all to see. The Pentagon had its former "war on terror" rebranded as The Long War; Dick Cheney swore that the genuine article will last for decades, a replay of the war between Eastasia and Oceania in Orwell's *1984*. George W. Bush had issued a "wild specula- tion" non-denial denial that the U.S. was planning strategic nuclear strikes against Iran. A "new Hitler"—but wasn't he Saddam Hussein in 1991 and then Saddam remixed in 2003?—had also been rebranded and his name was Mahmoud Ahmadinejad, the Iranian President, while the previous Hitler was still alive fighting—and then being sentenced to hang—by a kangaroo court in Baghdad.

Ahmadinejad was incessantly depicted by the ideological machine as an angry, totally irrational, Jew-hating, Holocaust-denying, Islamo-fascist who wanted to "wipe Israel off the map." The quote, repeated ad nauseam, came from an October 2005 speech. But what he really said, in Farsi, to an annual anti-Zionist conference in Iran, was that "the regime occupying Jerusalem must vanish from the page of time." He was actually quoting the Ayatollah Khomeini, who had said the same thing in the early 1980s. He was hoping that an unfair regime (towards Palestine) would be replaced by another one more equitable, not threatening to nuke Israel. It didn't matter. Just like in a Monty Python sketch the mob could not stop scream- ing "Witch! Witch!"

How does the leadership in Tehran analyze all this mess? Tactically, they see neocon Washington going no holds barred for regime change—as much as strategically they see it plunged in a take-no-prisoners war on Islam. The proof was the U.S./Israeli alliance in the summer of 2006 Lebanon war. Whatever the spin for world public opinion, nothing will convince the leadership in Tehran of the contrary. Eventual U.N. sanctions against Iran will never be as hardcore as the neocons would dream. No sanctions will force Iran to deviate from its civilian nuclear program. And then one fine day Iran masters enough technology to produce a nuclear bomb. This could certainly happen before the end of the second Bush administration, in January 2009.

What next? George W. Bush—who Gore Vidal calls "the little emperor"—vowed from the deep recesses of his soul that he would never allow Iran to become a nuclear power. It's another *Blues Brothers*-inspired Mission from God. So the march to mini-Armageddon may be inevitable. The only ones capable of stopping it would be sensible, rational, influential voices inside the U.S. military complex. Threats will proliferate. And then the White House decides that a preemptive nuclear strike—against a non-nuclear power—is a wiser decision than doing nothing. This Persian-American war would finally configure the U.S., for 1.5 billion Muslims, as *Dajjal,* a force of evil bent on destroying Islam. The dark side, no less. And against the dark side, all Islam would have to be united—Sunnis and Shiites. Traditional U.S. allies like Saudi Arabia, Pakistan, Egypt, the Gulf petromonarchies (their governments, not their populations) would not be afforded the luxury to sit on the fence: this would mean certain collapse. The Persian-American war could in fact realign the whole Arab-Muslim world. But not exactly the way mini-Armageddon stakeholders see it.

A Trilateral Commission Report presented in a meeting in Tokyo in the summer of 2006 proposes some sound solutions: direct U.S.-Iran negotiations leading to a Regional Middle East Nuclear Council where every declared (and some undeclared) nuclear powers would be represented:

U.S., Russia, China, France, the U.K., India, Pakistan, Iran, Israel and Japan. The IAEA would be allowed to inspect anything it wanted, with absolutely no restrictions. Israel would get a "security package" and Iran would be reassured of no regime change attempt. The Middle East and the Maghreb would get a sort of Marshall Plan: Palestine, Jordan, Tunisia, Morocco, Egypt and Algeria would join the WTO and get funds from the World Bank. A regional Middle East Water Council—including Turkey, Syria, Lebanon, Iraq, Israel, Palestine and Jordan—would also be implemented, as well as a Middle East Energy Council—including Saudi Arabia, the Emirates, Kuwait, Bahrain, Oman, Yemen, Iraq, and Iran—to take care of regional Pipelineistan, oil security, technology transfers.

Yes, it sounds too smooth to be true. And yes, many of these regimes are not exactly sure they want to be "helped" (or dictated by) the WTO and the Paul Wolfowitz-presided World Bank. This would be a case of the Greater Middle East being achieved not by the barrel of a gun but by "free trade"/market opening for Corporatistan. The marketing ploy would be slightly more sophisticated, and fewer lives would be lost, but the results would be substantially the same.

From the point of view of the Pentagon's Long War, a strategic nuclear attack on Iran has the obvious merit of being spun to oblivion as the crucial next stage of the war on "radical Islam." Buried in the militaristic rubble is the fact that Ayatollah Khomeini, the leader of the Islamic Revolution, had made clear in the 1980s that production, possession and use of nuclear weapons is against Islam. Russia, China, India, key E.U. players like Germany, and the overwhelming majority of the South still take him at his word. For the Iranian government, the nuclear program is a powerful symbol of independence vis-à-vis what is considered Anglo-Saxon colonialism. The view is shared by Iranians of all social classes and all educational backgrounds. Moreover, Iran is pushing for a leading role in the Non-Aligned Movement (NAM), stating that every country has the right to a peaceful nuclear program. What Iran officially wants is a nuclear-free zone in West Asia, and that of course includes Israel, the sixth nuclear power in the world with more than 600 nuclear warheads.

German philosopher Peter Sloterdijk seems to be closer to the mark when he says that "if tomorrow was unveiled a new technology which would end Western civilization's dependence on oil, the clash of civilizations would disappear overnight." We're quite far from it, hence The Long War.

The *Quadrennial Defense Review*—the Pentagon's strategic document which on 34 times, including the title, calls for a "Long War," a "Long, Global War" or a "Long, Irregular War" against terror can be interpreted even by an infant as a call for a war on Islam. The Iranian political elite is more than aware that Washington might release Shock and Awe remixed, including the possibility of unilateral nuclear bombing. The question is when. But everyone—reformists included—downplays the possibility of a street revolution toppling the nationalist theocracy, as the neocons' wishful thinking rules; in the event of a foreign attack virtually the whole population would rally behind the government.

Amid non-stop carpet info-bombing, it's easy for global citizens to forget that oil and gas had, once again, to be at the heart of the matter. Preventing the emergence of any strategic "rival," according to PNAC, means the U.S. exercising a sort of strategic veto over the E.U. and Japan in terms of control of energy. Thus the U.S. by all means needs to control Iran, Iraq, Saudi Arabia and Kuwait in the Middle East. Iraq will be a disaster zone for years, if not decades, and there's no guarantee the U.S. will control its oil reserves. Iran—since 1979—is absolutely off limits, the Big Prize.

From a PNAC/Pentagon point of view, the ultimate nightmare—very plausible in the short to medium term—would be the emergence of a loose alliance of Iran, the Shiite parties in power in Iraq and the Shiites in Hasa in Saudi Arabia controlling a very powerful axis of energy intimately linked to the Asian Energy Security Grid and under the protection of the Shanghai Cooperation Organization (SCO).

An article in the July 2006 issue of *Scientific American* by U.S. scientists affiliated with the U.S. Electric Power Research Institute suggests that a long term (22d Century) solution to global energy issues would be construction of a superconducting (supercold) grid for transmitting electricity around the globe. It's interesting that the article is accompanied by a 1981 map drawn by the polymath visionary Buckminster Fuller that illustrates a global pipeline route that avoids prolonged trips across oceans—and thus tracks very closely with the map of Eurasia. Such a project would require trillions of dollars (or euros!) of investment in highly vulnerable insulated pipeline, and a proportionately large investment in pipeline security—by *someone.*

For now, Iran is the absolutely crucial node of the proposed Asian Energy Security Grid, which includes China, Russia and India. This Grid would do nothing less than bypass Western—especially American—control of energy supplies in the Middle East/Central Asia arc and fuel a real 21st Century industrial revolution all across Asia. It's no wonder that scores of independent analysts in Iran, Pakistan, China, India and Russia view the U.S. war on Iran as essentially a war of the West against Asia. A surefire way to engender a coming conflict with China is to put its energy supply under threat. David Harvey from New York University and author of *The New Imperialism,* goes straight to the point: "Whoever controls the Middle East will control the global oil spigot, and who controls the global oil spigot will control the global economy, at least in the near future."

A war on Iran is a war against China. China created the SCO in June 2001—with Russia and the Central Asians Uzbekistan, Kazakhstan, Kyrgyzstan and Tajikistan as members. At first the SCO was basically a security arrangement to prevent terrorism although officially it was also promoting "cooperation in political affairs, economy and trade, scientific-technical, cultural, and educational spheres as well as in energy, transportation, tourism, and environment protection fields." It slowly evolved to a series of security, economic and infrastructure agreements, coupled with the odd, joint military exercise. By 2006 Iran, India, Pakistan and Mongolia had become participating observers. And Afghanistan, the CIS countries and the ASEAN 10 were visitors. All of them could become full members by 2007 or 2008. Thus the SCO, silent as a kung fu master, had suddenly blossomed as a kind of Asian answer to the E.U. and NATO.

It's very enlightening to contrast the SCO agenda—the wider Asian agenda, in short—with the PNAC/Pentagon worldview. According to its 2006 summit, the SCO:

"has outlined a new norm of international relations aiming at ensuring equal rights for all countries worldwide...a new and non-confrontational model...that calls for discarding the Cold War mentality and transcending ideological differences..."

"opposes interference in other countries' internal affairs, using the excuse of the differences in cultural traditions, political and social systems, values and models of development."

"safeguards each other's sovereignty, security and territorial integrity and in case of emergencies that threaten regional peace, stability and security, we will have immediate consultations and respond effectively to protect our member states."

"in economic cooperation [our goal] is to realize a free flow of goods, services, capital and technology by 2020 amongst members."

"holds that the next Secretary-General of the United Nations should come from Asia."

It's also very enlightening to superimpose the list of SCO members and soon-to-be members on the map of Eurasia. Virtually all the big players—with the exception of the U.S. "protectorates" Japan and South Korea—are represented.

The International Conference on Energy and Security: Asian Vision, held in Tehran in the spring of 2006, could not be a better place to examine how scholars and executives from Iran, China, Pakistan, India, Russia, Egypt, Indonesia, Georgia, Venezuela and Germany saw the future. The overall message was unmistakable: they see an interdependence of Asia and "Persian Gulf geo-ecopolitics," as an Iranian analyst put it. They want the U.S.-Iran nuclear row solved diplomatically. And they bet on Asian integration with Pipelineistan linking the Persian Gulf, Central Asia, South Asia and China.

This Persian Gulf/Asia interplay is more than enshrined. World demand for natural gas will triple from now to 2020. By 2025, Asia will import 80% of its total oil needs, and 80% of this total will be from the Persian Gulf. Chinese executives like Liu Guochen from the Sinochem Corp., based in Amman, admit that China will keep importing energy from unstable areas, and the Middle Kingdom will remain worried about "U.S. hegemony" over the flow of energy resources. That's why China is frantically diversifying, as Iranian scholar Masoud Akhavan-Kazemi of Razi University puts it, "in its investments, pursuing territorial claims and building up strategic oil reserves." He foresees Asia facing "great imbalances"; potential for conflict in the Persian Gulf, Russia, Central Asia and the Caspian; insecurity suffered by China, India and Japan vis-à-vis the U.S. drive in Asia; and a Chinese sense of vulnerability as China and the U.S. remain de facto strategic rivals.

Akhavan-Kazemi sees the U.S. pursuing three key objectives. The first two may be shared by some in Asia: guaranteeing the energy flows from Asia to international markets; and trying to stop Russian hegemony. But a crucial factor—which the Russians are keen to point out—is that Iran, India and Pakistan are now observers at the SCO. In the mid to short-term, as the organization develops, "the SCO would be able to protect pipelines going in all directions," says a Russian oil executive. As for the third American objective —preventing Iran from exporting its gas— definitely it is not shared by anyone. Akhavan-Kazemi emphasizes that "despite the

American military hegemony in the Persian Gulf, its political hegemony is in doubt."

Most Asian oil and gas executives and scholars agree that the way the game is played today in Pipelineistan, everything is politicized. "When Bush tells India you don't need to import gas from Iran, that's totally illogical," says Albert Bininachvili, a Georgian scholar based in Bologna. "The [alleged Iranian] bomb is a pretext," says Manouchehr Takin, a senior petroleum upstream analyst based in London. "The Americans don't want Iran to develop, and that's equally true of China and Venezuela. We need to talk about security through knowledge." To sum it all up, Asia does not want an Iran battered by the West; Iran, after all, is part of West Asia.

It took less than a decade for a full Eurasian swing since former National-al Security Adviser Zbigniew Brzezinski wrote his landmark 1997 piece "A Geostrategy for Eurasia," published by *Foreign Affairs*. Then, for Brzezinski, it was a question of formatting how to keep America's "global primacy" and "historical legacy" in "the decisive geopolitical chessboard." It was a time when America was still viewed as "the indispensable nation."

Brzezinski may be criticized for being "past his sell-by date," but it's important to follow his thinking through time for two reasons: he's a solid practitioner of *realpolitik*, as much as Henry Kissinger or Brent Scowcroft; and he's dedicated a lot of effort to formulate and publicly explain a U.S. Eurasian policy. A testament to the remarkable continuity of the American hegemonic project—irrespective of who is in power —is that Brzezinski's "swingin' into Eurasia" master plan was enthusiastically incorporated by PNAC, the subsequent Bush-Cheney system and U.S. Corporatistan. It was always clear that the implementation of Brzezinski's agenda would presuppose a Pentagon on a cocktail of steroids and vigilant, non-stop manufacture of internal consent—a state of affairs only arrived at after 9/11.

Brzezinski is a keen Mackinder disciple. Sir Halford John Mackinder (1861-1947) is the celebrated father of geopolitics who in 1902 introduced to the Royal Geographic Society his famous paper The *Geographic Pivot of*

History, where he developed the Heartland Theory. According to Mackinder the "world island" was Europe, Asia and Africa, and the "islands" were the Americas, Australia, the British Isles and Japan. The Heartland stretched from the Volga to the YangTze and from the Arctic to the Himalayas. The key for a true global power was to control Eurasia. As the Mackinder formula enunciated, "who rules East Europe commands the Heartland; who rules the Heartland commands the world-island; who rules the world-island controls the world."

Mackinder-drenched Brzezinski correctly stated in his piece that "all the historical pretenders to global power originated in Eurasia" (although, by another historical irony, the last two superpowers, the British Empire and the U.S., were "islands"). As "the world's axial super continent," any power in control of Eurasia "would exercise decisive influence over two of the world's three most economically productive regions, Western Europe and East Asia." This would answer Immanuel Wallerstein's question of which of the members of the Triad dominates the capitalist world system in the next phase.

Brzezinski wanted "the emergence of strategically compatible partners which, prompted by American leadership, might shape a more cooperative trans-Eurasian security system." Yet he could never have predicted the emergence of the SCO as a counter-power.

Brzezinski stated that "America's status as the world's premier power is unlikely to be contested by any single challenger for more than a generation. No state is likely to match the United States in the four key dimensions of power—military, economic, technological, and cultural—that confer global political clout." Yet the U.S. has been challenged in at least two—economic and technological. "Culture" means essentially pop culture—Hollywood, pop rock, TV series, reality shows—but global challenges abound, from world music to Bollywood, from world cinema to Mexican and Brazilian *telenovelas.* Wallerstein and Professor Eric Hobsbawm would argue that the only dimension of power left for the U.S. is the military. Brzezinski's dream of "a benign American hegemony" is gone.

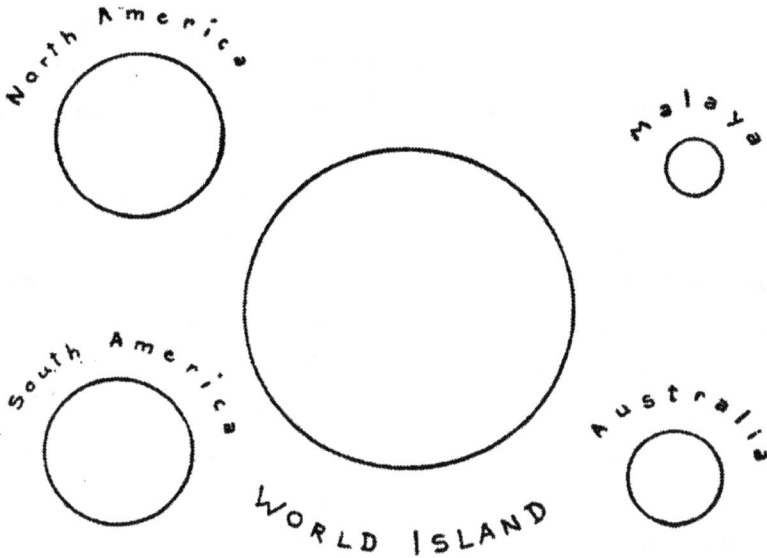

FIG. 12.—These circles represent the relative areas of the World-Island and its satellites.

Figure 2. Mackinder's abstract rendition of the relationship between the World Island and its satellites in Democratic Ideals and Reality (1919).

Brzezinski correctly noted "like insular Britain in the case of Europe, Japan is politically irrelevant to the Asian mainland." But he did not believe that China was likely to become a global dominant power for a long time. Brzezinski may have anticipated the Chinese demographic crisis caused by the one-child policy—the U.S., with its younger population and less stress on its "carrying capacity," is in a much better demographic position—but maybe he should review the Chinese economic data.

Brzezinski essentially dreamed of an emasculated E.U. "A larger Europe will expand the range of American influence without simultaneously creating a Europe so politically integrated that it could challenge the United States on matters of geopolitical importance, particularly in the Middle East." He was thinking in terms of a batch of new eastern European members eager to join NATO and benefit from E.U. cash, but not interested in integration. He was not thinking in terms of France and Germany, supported by Spain and Italy, working towards deepening European political integration.

America, for Brzezinski, "should also support Turkish aspirations to have a pipeline from Baku, Azerbaijan, to Ceyhan on its own Mediterranean coast [to] serve as a major outlet for the Caspian sea basin energy reserves." The result was the Baku-Tblisi-Ceyhan (BTC) pipeline, of which Brzezinski himself was a major instigator.

But the crucial point still is what Brzezinski, a *realpolitik* practitioner, had to say about Iran. The solution, for him, definitely was not Shock and Awe. "It is not in America's interest to perpetuate U.S.-Iranian hostility. Any eventual reconciliation should be based on both countries' recognition of their mutual strategic interest in stabilizing Iran's volatile regional environment. A strong, even religiously motivated—but not fanatically anti-Western— Iran is still in the U.S. interest. American long-range interests in Eurasia would be better served by abandoning existing U.S. objections to closer Turkish-Iranian economic cooperation, especially in the construction of new pipelines from Azerbaijan and Turkmenistan. In fact, American financial participation in such projects would be to America's benefit."

Brzezinski dreamed of the U.S. having a "decisive role as Eurasia's arbitrator." Eurasia's stability, in his view, "would be enhanced by the emergence, perhaps early in the next century, of a trans-Eurasian security system. Such a transcontinental security arrangement might involve an expanded NATO, linked by cooperative security agreements with Russia, China, and Japan. But to get there, Americans and Japanese must first set in motion a triangular political-security dialogue that engages China." Forget about an expanded NATO. Forget about Japan engaging China. The future of Eurasia seems to be spelling "SCO" plus Asian Energy Security Grid.

Cue to 9 years later. Nathan Gardels, editor-in-chief of a journal of social and political thought published by Global Services of the Los Angeles Times Syndicate/Tribune, asks Brzezinski whether military superiority leads to eternal enmity or to more security. Brzezinski's answer could not be more *realpolitik*: "The lessons of Iraq speak for themselves. Eventually, if neocon policies continue to be pursued, the United States will be expelled from the region and that will be the beginning of the end for Israel as well."

Brzezinski refined his new worldview—but up to a point—in a September 2006 interview with Germany's *Der Spiegel*. He admitted we were now in a historic stage of "global political awakening" in which "people in China and India, but also in Nepal, in Bolivia or Venezuela will no longer tolerate the enormous disparities in the human condition." But he framed this upheaval not in terms of a global struggle for a more equitable system, but in terms of a collective *danger*, a "challenge to global stability." Irrepressibly the hegemonic, he still viewed "the American leadership role vulnerable, but irreplaceable in the foreseeable future." Well, let's plunge into liquid modernity—or "space-velocity," as French cross-cultural analyst Paul Virilio put it—and see for ourselves.

To purchase Globalistan, *go to your favorite online bookseller or ask your local bookstore to order a copy via Ingram. The ISBN is 0978813820.*

Publisher Information

AMAZON UPGRADE

If you purchased this book from Amazon.com, you can acquire online access via Amazon Upgrade. There is a link in the Your Account section of Amazon.com, or (usually) in the top right corner of the Amazon detail page for this book.

ORDERING THIS BOOK IN QUANTITY

Copies may be purchased in quantity (2 or more) for 35% off list, plus shipping and handling; prepayment required.

ABOUT NIMBLE BOOKS

Our trusty Merriam-Webster Collegiate Dictionary defines "nimble" as follows:

> *1: quick and light in motion: AGILE *nimble fingers**
>
> *2 a: marked by quick, alert, clever conception, compre-hension, or resourcefulness *a nimble mind* b: RESPONSIVE, SENSITIVE *a nimble listener**

And traces the etymology to the 14th Century:

> *Middle English nimel, from Old English numol holding much, from niman to take; akin to Old High German neman to take, Greek nemein to distribute, manage, nomos pasture, nomos usage, custom, law*

The etymology is reminiscent of the old Biblical adage, "to whom much is given, much is expected" (Luke 12:48). Nimble Books seeks to honor that Christian principle by combining the spirit of *nimbleness* with the Biblical concept of *abundance:* we deliver what you need to know about a subject in a quick, resourceful, and sensitive manner.

Why Publish With Nimble Books

Nimble Books LLC is an innovative publisher of timely material on topics ranging from Iraq and politics to Harry Potter and Dan Brown. We use electronic publishing technology to reach markets that are moving too fast for the large publishing conglomerates to address. Because our marketing strategy is tightly focused on the Internet, we look for titles that respond well to keyword searching in on-line markets, or on-line promotion via blogging.

We publish twelve titles per year and we are selective. We are looking for books that are substantially ahead of the curve in that they address emerging trends that are readily connected with large, literate on-line communities.

If you like what you see here and you have something similar on the shelf, or in the works, please visit the Nimble Books website and take a look at "Why Publish With Us" (http://www.nimblebooks.com/wordpress/why-publish-with-nimble-books/). Then send a proposal and sample chapters to wfz@nimblebooks.com.

Colophon

This book was produced using Microsoft Word 2007 and Adobe Acrobat 8.1. The cover was produced using The Gimp 2.0.2 with Ghostscript.

Heading fonts, the body text, and quotations are in Constantia.